In Peace and Freedom

In Peace and Freedom

My Journey in Selma

Bernard LaFayette Jr.
and
Kathryn Lee Johnson

Foreword by
Congressman John Robert Lewis

Afterword by
Raymond Arsenault

UNIVERSITY PRESS OF KENTUCKY

Scholarly publisher for the Commonwealth,
serving Bellarmine University, Berea College, Centre College of Kentucky,
Eastern Kentucky University, The Filson Historical Society, Georgetown
College, Kentucky Historical Society, Kentucky State University, Morehead
State University, Murray State University, Northern Kentucky University,
Transylvania University, University of Kentucky, University of Louisville,
and Western Kentucky University.
All rights reserved.

Editorial and Sales Offices: The University Press of Kentucky
663 South Limestone Street, Lexington, Kentucky 40508-4008
www.kentuckypress.com

17 16 15 14 13   5 4 3 2 1

Cataloging-in-Publication data is available from the Library of Congress.

ISBN 978-0-8131-4386-6 (hardcover : alk. paper)
ISBN 978-0-8131-4434-4 (epub)
ISBN 978-0-8131-4435-1 (pdf)

This book is printed on acid-free paper meeting the requirements of the
American National Standard for Permanence in Paper for Printed Library
Materials.

Manufactured in the United States of America.

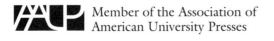 Member of the Association of
American University Presses

To the four women who have most influenced my life:
Rozelia Forrester,
Verdell LaFayette,
Amelia Boynton,
and Kate Bulls LaFayette

Contents

Illustrations follow page 90

Foreword

In this book, Bernard LaFayette Jr. has written a powerful history of struggle, commitment, and hope. No one, but no one, who lived through the creation and development of the movement for voting rights in Selma is better prepared to tell this story than Bernard LaFayette himself. He was trained in nonviolence by a master, the Reverend Jim Lawson, and stood shoulder to shoulder with Dr. Martin Luther King Jr. He was the Student Nonviolent Coordinating Committee's main organizer in Selma. This book fills in many blanks left by other discussions and research on the struggle for the right to vote in modern American history.

Through the lens of his training in the philosophy and the discipline of nonviolence and his commitment to social and political change, Bernard LaFayette takes us on a journey through the heart of the Deep South and the Black Belt of Alabama. He makes the story of the struggle real; he makes it come alive.

It is fitting that this book will be published as we approach the commemoration of the fiftieth anniversary of the March from Selma to Montgomery. This work highlights not just why we needed to take action but also why the Voting Rights Act of 1965 was long overdue. The marches and protests in Selma were necessary. They disturbed an unjust peace and paved the way for justice. They dramatized the need for a mandate to protect the right to vote of every citizen in Alabama, throughout the South, and throughout America.

This book also helps us process the lessons of the recent election of 2012, where voting and voting rights were the center of debate. At the time of this writing, the Supreme Court is considering the constitutionality of Section 5 of the Voting Rights Act. As they deliberate, this book will serve as a necessary guide for citizens, students, and scholars.

John Robert Lewis
United States House of Representatives

Preface

Ever since I was a teenager I have had an interest in civil rights. I participated in the Youth Council of the National Association for the Advancement of Colored People (NAACP) in Tampa, Florida, at an early age. In Tampa the president of the NAACP was Rev. Leon Lowry and the field secretary was Mr. Robert Sanders. But my active involvement in the civil rights movement began when I was a student at the American Baptist Theological Seminary in Nashville, Tennessee. My roommate, John Robert Lewis from Troy, Alabama (who was later elected U.S. Representative from Atlanta, Georgia), persuaded me to attend some nonviolence workshops conducted by Rev. James Lawson. I was preoccupied with my studies and jobs on campus and felt I was too busy to take on another obligation. However, after going to one meeting I was convinced that working toward nonviolence and peace would become one of my life's missions.

What fascinated me about Rev. Lawson's approach was the clear connection between our biblical and theological studies and the social change movement. Up to that point I had not seen the connection. This was a turning point in my life where I combined the gospel with the social change movement based on the concept of love from New Testament theology. I was curious to learn more.

My introduction to Gandhi and learning about the powerful nonviolent movements he led were life changing for me. I began to see the relationship, connection, and symmetry between Gandhi's movement in a country on the other side of the world and our movement of social change right here in the United States. I was inspired, just as Dr. King was, by the possible impact that nonviolence could have in this country. The most important aspect was that it had immediate practical application, not just intellectual curiosity. The idea of civil disobedience intrigued me as I came to understand that it was more important to obey a moral law than an unjust civil law. The fact that a foreign country could have experienced a similar situation in struggling for civil rights made me realize that nonviolence is universal.

I was fascinated with the methods Lawson used in teaching, particularly role play and social drama. We set up the situations we might encounter and practiced our responses to them. The other concept that captivated me was how people's emotions significantly affect their behavior. Emotions are always present, and if we allow them to gain control, we can move in the wrong direction. If we find the strength to discipline our emotions, this can serve as a catalyst for guiding our own behavior in a positive direction. Lawson strung together many different threads into one woven philosophy. And I wrapped myself up in this cloth.

Most important was the personal challenge to bring out the best of myself. While I had studied the scriptures and the concept of love—loving your enemy and doing good to those who mistreat you—I was internalizing how moral behavior could be a force for change. Changing the relationship with others, particularly our adversaries, was part of the strategy of nonviolence. The Nashville workshops were designed to help us embrace others as individual human beings, and also to learn how the same moral force could be used to change the attitudes of an entire community. These workshops emphasized not only interpersonal change but systemic change. It was a personal experimentation as I grasped these new ideas, not just intellectually but by living them each day. The practice of learning to love people who had literally put their foot in my face was a challenge. I could take the blows physically without retaliating, but the question was whether or not I could muster up enough emotional feeling to actually love those people. I came to understand that if I were to reach the goal I was seeking, I needed to accept the suffering. The goal was to win those people over and to help bring out the best in other people, so I had to present the best in myself. I had to be the example that I wanted them to see.

Nashville became a laboratory for me. I liked collaborating with others in a collegial way where decisions were made by consensus. I got caught up in the movement, and it became the most important thing in my life because it meant I was doing something concrete. The practical results were changing the segregation system. It was also a way to test my convictions as to whether I was willing to stand up for something I believed in. The New Testament spoke about people who went to jail for their beliefs, such as Jesus, Paul, and Silas, who stood up against an unjust system. I knew I was in good company. Another difficulty was overcoming fear in order to do what was right and accept the consequences, not knowing what they would be. I chose to live in the moment and make decisions that would affect my entire life, such as getting a jail record or being crippled by an attack. I lived not knowing what the coming days would hold but having faith that my actions at any moment could change my future forever.

Abbreviations

AME	African Methodist Episcopal
CORE	Congress of Racial Equality
NAACP	National Association for the Advancement of Colored People
SCLC	Southern Christian Leadership Conference
SNCC	Student Nonviolent Coordinating Committee
SRC	Southern Regional Council

Prologue

The Road into Selma, Fall 1962

Traveling to Selma to visit the town where I would spend the next couple of years, I drove west on Highway 80, winding my way through the peaceful hills of Lowndes County, Alabama. The noon sun of this November day shone across vast stretches of farmland, dotted with giant rolls of hay, freshly harvested. I saw open pastures scattered with farmhouses, noticing how each farm was divided by rows of trees, and how the browning kudzu covered dying branches. Traveling the gently rolling hills and rounding the curves was like lifting the veils off a new picture along this ever-changing highway.

Suddenly, sirens pierced the air and flashing lights jolted me from faraway thoughts. A long streak of black tire marks marred the road. An overturned feed truck and an old car lodged in a ditch had police officers and an emergency team scrambling around in chaos. Yellow-gold feed, spilled from the demolished grain truck, covered the ground and highway. I pulled onto the shoulder to help. Medics worked feverishly to give oxygen to the truck driver, who was hanging upside down in the cab, his head a bloody mop. They were twisting and turning his bleeding body to remove him from the crushed front seat. But it was too late.

A gray-haired black man stood at the side of the road, his head gashed. Blood flowed down his face and dripped onto his body. Although he was injured, the medics completely ignored him. He was talking to two policemen and looking nervous, eyes on the ground. Behind him in the ditch was his battered black car, early 1950s, with the back end smashed. He explained what had happened, describing the accident. He said that the huge open-bed truck, overloaded with feed, had barreled over the steep hill behind him. Apparently, when the truck approached his slower-moving car going downhill, it had too much momentum to

1

stop. When the grain truck driver attempted to veer around the car, he clipped the rear end, knocking the black man's vehicle over an embankment. The grain truck screeched and careened off the road, somersaulted, and landed upside down, the white driver trapped inside.

The police officers were discussing whether or not to charge the black man with reckless driving. Even though it was his car that had been hit, they figured that he was somehow responsible. It was clear to me before I had even crossed into the city limits that blacks in Selma felt totally powerless in situations with white people. There was so much fear that they became immobilized. I used the information I gathered from this event to learn as much as I could about why Selma was such a devastating place for blacks.

Although I didn't realize it at the time, this incident was indicative of the deep-seated racial conflict that was present in this small Alabama town. Furthermore, it foreshadowed the many controversies and tragedies that were to come in my next two years of living in Selma.

1

Preparing for Selma

Peace is not merely a distant goal that we seek, but a means by which
we arrive at that goal.
                                        —Dr. Martin Luther King Jr.

Selma, Alabama. What was it about this little southern town that sparked
the question from so many people, "Why go to Selma? You can't bring
about any change there." I wondered about this sentiment as I made
plans to spend the next couple of years there as director of the Alabama
Voter Registration Campaign for the Student Nonviolent Coordinating
Committee (SNCC, commonly referred to as "snick"). The Southern
Regional Council's (SRC) "Voter Education Project," headed by Randolph Blackwell, was a recipient of grants from the Field Foundation
and Taconic Foundation. The foundation sponsored projects aimed at
increasing the number of voters in primarily black-populated counties
throughout Alabama, Mississippi, Arkansas, and Georgia. The SRC was
an organization founded in 1919 that was committed to fighting for
racial justice and informing public policy on issues of democratic rights
and equality.

President John F. Kennedy's administration had an influence in funding the voting project—"deliverables," as they called the funding. Because
Kennedy was elected unquestionably by the marginal votes from blacks,
his administration was committed to increasing support to help blacks
vote. In his inaugural address President Kennedy said, "We observe today
not a victory of party but a celebration of freedom—symbolizing an end
as well as a beginning—signifying renewal as well as change," and he also
quoted from the Bible the command to "undo the heavy burdens . . .
(and) let the oppressed go free."[1]

President Kennedy's address gave the black people in America hope.

3

His leadership inspired and motivated a new generation of blacks to press for change since we had White House support for the first time. I met President Kennedy while he was campaigning in New York. I was at a SNCC meeting and our entire group went to hear him speak. After the speech he shook our hands and gave SNCC recognition and support. So I felt a personal connection with this young president. The way that he spoke out for civil rights and recognized Dr. King authenticated what the movement was doing. Although many black citizens had lived in segregation in second-class conditions, now, as a result of President Kennedy's stand against discrimination, we felt that we were doing the right thing, the real American way. We were ready to continue our struggle, to accomplish as much as possible under President Kennedy's leadership.

Many southern blacks had two pictures on the wall, one of Jesus and one of Kennedy. Even though most were Baptists, they didn't care that Kennedy was Catholic. His voting record on civil rights as a senator was not strong, but he did recognize that blacks were supporting him and he looked at ways to gain more black votes.

I felt that Kennedy, as president of the United States, should advocate for the idea of the government as a democracy of the people and for the people. It is the president's responsibility to take action to remove those impediments that prevent citizens, particularly disenfranchised people, from participating in government. Kennedy certainly voiced his support to protect those rights, most memorably in his speech "Ask not what your country can do for you, but what you can do for your country." He challenged us as young people to have a commitment. As a civil rights activist, I never considered myself a rebel against the nation, never anti-American. I was proud of my country and wanted to work to help it be the best, and for it to live up to its creed and purpose. I felt what I was doing was of service to my country. I would have volunteered in the military, and I considered becoming a chaplain in the air force. However, the nonviolence movement gave me a better way to serve my country, a positive way, a more peaceful way.

At the end of the summer of 1962, I went to get my assignment as director of a campaign from James Forman, the executive secretary of SNCC, at the SNCC headquarters in Atlanta. I had spent the previous two years participating in Nashville lunch counter sit-ins, riding buses across the south as a Freedom Rider, and working with the Jackson Mississippi Nonviolent Movement, and I was editor of the Jackson movement newsletter. I had always had a great respect for Jim and recognized that he was effective in his work with SNCC. He had maturity and experience, and most important, he had a great rapport with students. He knew the importance of students taking leadership to challenge injustices and to bring about change. Not only was he an administrator but he joined us on the front line because of his personal passion for the cause. He was a leader who truly forged the way. In some instances Jim was more radical than the students. He had both the southern experience of Mississippi and the northern exposure of Chicago.

That day Jim told me, "I'm sorry, Bernard, but we don't have any directorships available at this time."

I simply couldn't believe that all the directorships had been assigned, especially since Jim knew I was waiting for one. I said, "Now Jim, remember I helped to raise the $30,000 bond money for three SNCC workers." Dion Diamond, Chuck McDew, and Bob Zellner were in jail in Louisiana for helping blacks register to vote. I had been sent to Detroit and Chicago to raise money to help get them released. "You promised me a directorship position when I returned, but now you're insisting that nothing is available? This isn't right."

He said, "You could work with Charles Sherrod in southwest Georgia, Bob Moses in Mississippi, or Bill Hansen in Arkansas." Even though I was only twenty-two, I was determined and made it clear, stating emphatically, "I don't want to be an assistant director. I'm ready to be a director of a project and you should keep your promise."

Jim said, "Bernard, the only project left is the Alabama Voter Registration Campaign in Selma, but we just removed Selma from the list. So it's out of the question. Two groups of SNCC workers just returned from scouting the city and reported, 'The white folks are too mean and the black folks are too afraid.'"

Despite the fact that the town was centrally located in Alabama, SNCC marked a bold black X across Selma on the wall map of the state. However, Jim said, "Even though we've rejected Selma, if you want to, you can go there, check it out, and see what you think." Alabama was infamous for the suppression of black voting rights, and with its central location and large numbers of blacks, Selma seemed to me like the perfect place to headquarter the state office for voter registration.

I enthusiastically responded, "I'll take Selma, sight unseen." That is how I became director of the Alabama Voter Registration Campaign. I was searching for a place and Selma had potential, with all the ingredients for a successful movement. We never randomly chose a location; we were strategic about selecting certain criteria that indicated a movement could succeed. There were four elements that Dr. King believed would lead to a movement's success: (1) it must have a distinct beginning and end; (2) it should focus on a local problem that could gain national attention about a more global issue; (3) activists must be trained in nonviolent strategies; and (4) attitudes of the local community must be transformed. These four components were present in the Montgomery Bus Boycott, and I believed that these could be achieved in Selma.

I had a little time before going to Selma to educate myself about the conditions there and to plan a strategy. My first step to prepare for the campaign was to research the city of Selma to understand why there were such negative attitudes in Dallas County that they caused SNCC workers to conclude, "Nothing can happen in Selma." I studied nonstop for a solid week at the Tuskegee Institute (now Tuskegee University) Library and stayed with Mrs. Lois Reeves, who was head of the "Y" on Tuskegee's campus, and her daughter, Cookie. My exploration focused on newspaper clippings, Census Bureau reports, and other reference books, as I tried to piece together a picture of Selma. I even found a periodical of the White Citizen's Council, a white supremacy group. It was filled with helpful information in learning how this group thought.

I was struck by the complacency of the black citizens and their unknowing complicity in supporting the existing oppressive system. I didn't know what I would find as I went down this road. Not only did I have a strong curiosity, but I had a strong determination to do whatever I could to turn the situation around. There was never a doubt in my mind that change would eventually come. At the time I had not anticipated a national Voting Rights Act, but I had a specific mission to change Dallas County, Alabama.

Although I didn't have a preconceived plan, my overall goals, principles, and strategies arose from my Nashville lunch counter sit-in experiences, from the Freedom Rides, and from my Grandmama, Ma Foster. Not knowing what I would encounter, I knew it wouldn't be easy. I was not naive, and it was clear that I wouldn't be able to take on this daunting task alone.

In my research, I learned about the economic and political history, and that Selma was the site of one of the last battles of the Civil War. I noted the incidents of lynchings and other events that discouraged people from trying to exercise their constitutional right to vote. I discovered that only 156 of Dallas County's 15,000 blacks of voting age were registered to vote. While the counties in that area were more than half black, only about 1 percent of blacks were registered to vote. There were long, intimidating application forms to complete and nearly impossible literacy tests to pass. In addition, the applicants had to have a registered voter to vouch for them, which was difficult to find. Often it was random whether or not someone would pass the exams; it depended on the whim of the registrar.

I discovered that the capital of Alabama from 1820 to 1826 had been Cahawba, located southwest of Selma, now a ghost town and historic site. When Cahawba flooded, the capital was moved to Montgomery. I heard whites from Dallas County comment from time to time that politicians "stole our capital" and that moving the capital had never been forgiven. The battleship *Buchanan* was built on the banks of the Alabama River in Dallas County. The county also had a large volunteer force in the Civil War. So Selma was no small potato; there were deep roots in its struggle. It was necessary to understand the history of the town and be aware of what I was walking into.

I sensed that there was a feeling of inferiority on the part of many white individuals in Selma. Many questions flooded my mind. Could it be that they were humiliated that they couldn't keep their capital in Dallas County? Could this account for the rigidity they had in their efforts to show strength by keeping black people "in their place"? How did this affect the personality of Selma? Communities have personalities, just like people. I needed to learn about how the people there perceived themselves and others. What caused these oppressive conditions to be perpetuated? I was puzzled why SNCC, a strong, fearless group that would go anywhere, backed away from Selma. For a long time it has been my belief that it is not experiences themselves that drive people to behave a certain way as much as their interpretation of the experiences. How would I interpret the fearful outlook of the blacks and the vicious attitude of the whites that created this pervasive violent climate? At this point I had more questions than answers.

It was important to learn about the social conditions in Selma in order to understand the contributing factors that created the problem. I knew that my job would be to focus on the source of the problem rather than dealing with the symptoms. To get a picture of the present status of Selma, I looked deeper at the community's response to recent events, such as desegregating their schools. The 1955 *Brown II* Supreme Court decision ruled that district courts would oversee school desegregation with "all deliberate speed."[2] In Selma the local citizens had to petition the school board with at least ten signatures for them to consider desegregating the schools. However, of those who signed in favor, I learned that all but one was forced to remove his signature from the petition. This was an oppressive and threatening power. People were being run out of town and family members were getting fired from their jobs. The one exception, Mr. Ernest Doyle, who was a federal employee with the U.S. Post Office in Selma, was the only petitioner whose job was secure. Yet he was not satisfied with the conditions in Selma, especially those conditions that severely affected others. He was somewhat of a quiet person, but he had no problem speaking up when he had something important to contribute. Unfortunately, there weren't enough signatures on the petition to go forward with a lawsuit by the NAACP.

While I was researching Selma in the library I noticed another man looking at the same documents. Using a large, sophisticated camera, he was photographing newspaper articles about lynchings. This man was Ralph Ginzburg from New York, who later wrote a book titled *100 Years of Lynchings*.

My findings were compiled into a fifty-page paper, which in part analyzed the economic conditions, or what we called "the hidden power structure." I discovered that eight families controlled Dallas County and held various leadership positions, including board members of banks, a table company, and the newspaper. That entire history was crucial to understanding why there was a psychological barrier between blacks and whites, with a strong consensus that nothing was going to change.

I thought it was interesting to study about the French general the Marquis de Lafayette, who was a prominent figure in the French and American Revolutions and who went through Selma and put that town on the map. I hoped to be the second LaFayette to make a mark on Selma.

When I made the decision to accept the position in Selma, I gave no thought to whether I would live or die. I was already convinced that it was a dangerous and life-threatening place. There was no pressure to have marches, demonstrations, or visible activity in the streets, so to speak, because nothing was really expected of me. The leaders at SNCC headquarters in Atlanta believed that it was a near impossible situation. However, I viewed it as possible. When I undertook this challenge I felt that some positive change could happen if we took the scientific approach learned through my previous activist education and applied a strategy connected to those findings. Our organizing strategy would have to focus on changing the attitude of fear and hopelessness on the part of blacks before any action could occur.

As I thought about the history of Selma I wondered how I would fit into that small town. Knowing that each movement was influenced by previous successes, I remembered a number of significant accomplishments in the area of social change before my arrival. These were *Brown v. Board of Education,* the Montgomery Bus Boycott, the lunch counter sit-ins, the Freedom Rides, and the formation of SNCC. I was actively involved in three of these, which prepared me to assume the leadership role of the Alabama Voter Registration Campaign. I examined how my knowledge from those previous movements might lead me to the most effective approach to working there.

The most recent movement I had been involved in was the Freedom Rides of 1961, a pivotal experience for me as I had become more immersed in civil rights activism. What impressed me the most was the deep courage and unwavering commitment from each rider. This was the first movement where a large number of activists from the North and other parts of the country came down to participate in a direct action campaign in the Deep South. The more I became involved in the Freedom Rides, the more I learned about the legal background that included several previous cases. Many people are unaware that the Freedom Rides were part of a series of protests that occurred across a number of years.

First, the *Morgan v. Commonwealth of Virginia* case of 1946 involved a young woman, Irene Morgan, who refused to give up her seat to a white passenger on a crowded Greyhound bus, several years before the Rosa Parks incident. At that time the Jim Crow laws in Virginia mandated segregated seating on public transportation vehicles. Irene Morgan was ejected from the bus, arrested, and convicted of violating the segregated seating law. NAACP lawyers took her case, and it went all the way up to the U.S. Supreme Court, which struck down the Virginia law of segregated seating on interstate transportation.[3] Yet even though this was a ruling from the highest court in the land, this decision was largely ignored and unenforced because of the ingrained Jim Crow traditions and racist attitudes. The 1947 Freedom Rides happened in the wake of this landmark case, when sixteen people (eight blacks and eight whites) boarded a Trailways bus to travel across four southern states to challenge the Jim Crow laws. The Rides resulted in unprovoked arrests.[4]

Another case that helped to set the stage for the 1961 Freedom Rides was *Boynton v. Virginia,* of 1960, where the U.S. Supreme Court ruled that segregation was unconstitutional in interstate facilities for travelers, such as bus terminals, public restrooms, and restaurants. It was based on the incident in which Bruce Boynton, a young law student from Selma, was arrested in Richmond at a Trailways terminal for attempting to eat in a white-only restaurant and refusing to leave. The Court ruled in favor of Boynton, deciding that restaurants in terminals cannot discriminate against customers according to race. By rendering this decision, the Court was really broadening the *Morgan* case. Once again, though, this decision was not enforced. However, this case grew in importance, as it led directly to the Freedom Rides of 1961.[5]

These Supreme Court cases pointed the way to the strategy of using a legal point of challenge. The Freedom Rides of 1961 were planned for mixed races and both genders to test the federal integration laws on the interstate bus routes across the South. Black and white passengers were to ride together on public buses from Washington, D.C., to New Orleans, challenging the racial segregation customs on the buses and in the bus terminals. White passengers would ride in the back of the bus and black passengers would ride in the front of the bus in seats usually reserved for white riders. It was agreed that black passengers would go into the white-only bus terminal restaurants and waiting rooms.

When two buses left on May 4, 1961, they met with violence outside of Anniston, Alabama, where one bus, a Greyhound, was fire-bombed by the Ku Klux Klan. Many riders were injured and beaten as they escaped the burning bus. The second bus, a Trailways, continued to Birmingham, where riders were attacked and brutally beaten. The Freedom Rides were temporarily halted because of the violence. The Freedom Riders wanted to continue; however, bus drivers refused to drive. Our SNCC members from the Nashville Student Movement agreed that the Freedom Rides should not be stopped by violence and should continue. A group of us dropped out of college in the midst of our final exams and, undaunted, continued the trip. Despite threats, beatings, and jail time, more than sixty bus rides continued through September with the participation of over four hundred riders. The Freedom Rides brought much national attention to the problems faced by black Americans in the South. This campaign eventually brought about significant new Interstate Commerce Commission rules that prohibited segregation in interstate travel.

The first time I ever heard about Selma was about a year and a half before I was assigned to go there to direct the campaign. In May 1961 I was on the Freedom Rides. We were journeying from Montgomery to Jackson, Mississippi. In the Montgomery bus station a ranting mob viciously attacked us. Several of us were severely beaten. However, we defied all expectations. We didn't run, we didn't fight back. We got back up when slammed to the ground, and looked our attackers directly in the eyes, fighting violence with nonviolence. In spite of our injuries, with many of us bleeding and battered, we got back on the bus and continued our ride toward Jackson. As we approached a small rural city about fifty miles from Montgomery, it was reported that an angry, armed mob of more than two thousand people waited for us at the bus station. That was Selma, Alabama. The bus company detoured our bus to avoid going through Selma, as it was too dangerous to stop there. A decoy bus was sent into Selma to distract and disperse the mob. It was thought that some of the Selma mob had driven to Montgomery earlier and were part of the ferocious attacking mob there. There was a young man on the bus that day, not a Freedom Rider, just a passenger, who said, "Mama said there'd be days like this." His mama was right.

Considering the massive number of hateful individuals appearing at the bus station, it was reasonable to assume that an overwhelming group of people in Selma would resist any attempt at change. They were not a small ragtag group. Even for a bus just passing through they were able to muster a sizable mob. It's not surprising that the blacks in Selma felt the pervasive negative attitude toward change from white people.

The second major impact on me was the lunch counter sit-ins in Greensboro, North Carolina, in 1960. Four black students sat down at a lunch counter in a Woolworth's store where they served only white customers. After they were refused service, they continued to sit at the counter, challenging the custom. This event led to other sit-ins around the country, including our own successful Nashville sit-ins of local lunch counters, which eventually led to desegregated eating facilities. These sit-ins introduced another type of direct action, where people put themselves in a position knowing they would be arrested. This was a difficult concept for me to digest at first because I was taught to be an obedient, law-abiding citizen. I learned that if you don't like certain laws, you should challenge them through the legal process in court. Dr. King had said for us not to obey unjust laws, and this was what we were doing—refusing to abide by unjust laws. John Lewis was another early advocate of going to and staying in jail as a form of protest. SNCC had publicly taken a stand to support the radical idea of "jail, no bail" in 1961 when they sent a delegation to North Carolina Agricultural and Technical College to join student sit-in demonstrators in jail.

Being arrested as part of a strategy to bring about change was a new concept for the movement. Before this, the force of the movement had been legal confrontation, and breaking the law was the impetus to the legal battle. But this unique shift brought about by Dr. King was creating a battle by first breaking the law, then filling the jails, and creating social dislocation as a means of challenging the system. Massive civil disobedience became popularized during the widespread sit-in movement. What was remarkable were the risks people were taking, with consequences that might follow them the rest of their lives. It seemed like an oxymoron that students who had worked hard to get into college for an education were sacrificing their educational opportunity by risking a jail record, which could have implications for future jobs. Yet this is exactly what we did.

The third significant influence was my involvement with SNCC, which was the key organization for student leaders from college campuses all over the South. We met to convene and discuss nonviolent strategy and direct action, and this connection led me to working with Dr. King. The committee was a vital part of my life from its inception. In 1960 Miss Ella Baker was working as an executive staff member for the Southern Christian Leadership Conference (SCLC), a civil rights organization that Miss Baker had helped to initiate in 1957 along with a group of activists, including Dr. King, its first president. Following the Greensboro sit-ins, Miss Baker met with the student leaders. Out of that meeting sprung the idea for SNCC. Miss Baker realized the meaning and potential of the sit-in movement as it swept the South, and she organized a national conference on Easter weekend at her alma mater, Shaw University in Raleigh, North Carolina. She encouraged students to attend this conference, which was cosponsored by SCLC, the NAACP, and the Congress of Racial Equality (CORE). These three national organizations often sponsored workshops and collaborated in hosting national conferences. James Farmer and others founded CORE in 1942 in Chicago, and its mission was to use nonviolent civil disobedience as a tactic to challenge racial segregation.[6] Jim called me "Little Gandhi" because I was small and skinny like Gandhi and believed so wholly in nonviolence. The thing that impressed me most about Jim was his respect for other civil rights leaders. He was never in competition but always sought ways to collaborate and form coalitions. He was the essence of inclusion.

Although SCLC had thought of SNCC as a youth affiliate and initially funded it, the students insisted on being autonomous rather than being part of the official structure of any national organization. After the Shaw conference, when a temporary student nonviolent coordinating committee was established, Marion Barry, a future mayor of Washington, D.C., who was then a student at Nashville's Fisk University, was elected SNCC's first national chairman. Based in Atlanta, SNCC became the most active and effective student civil rights organization of its time. Miss Baker and Constance Curry served as our first advisers.[7]

Miss Baker became a guide for me, as well as for many of the young leaders of the civil rights movement. She made students feel like mature leaders rather than radical youth. Although she was a small woman, she had a strong, deep, booming voice, which made her a powerful speaker. She used the Socratic method to help us think more strategically about the process of decision making and usually began her speeches with "Why are we here . . ." Her interest and involvement went back to her early years when she listened to her grandmother tell enthralling stories about slave revolts. Miss Baker had graduated from Shaw University at the top of her class in 1927. While a student, she challenged unfair school policies and strived to bring about change. A natural leader, she organized several activist groups, mostly focused on economic justice. As a staff member with the NAACP, Miss Baker organized more chapters in the South than any other person. She held a strong belief that young people have the energy and dedication to bring about social change, and SNCC provided the support and impetus for college activists. Miss Baker had the insight to promote "group-centered leaders" rather than the typical "leader-centered groups," which I took to heart and put to good use in Selma. This structure encouraged the leaders to emerge from the community and gave support to local organizations to help defeat oppression. I never saw her anxious about anything; she was a fortress of courage, yet her most endearing quality was her deep love for people. And all of us had a deep love for her.[8]

The other SNCC adviser who had a significant impact on many of us was Connie Curry. Connie grew up in Greensboro, North Carolina, and in the 1950s attended Agnes Scott College, a small all-white college for girls in Atlanta, Georgia. In spite of her conservative surroundings, and the fact that everything was segregated by law, she was interested in civil rights and racial issues and became friends with several student leaders at black colleges in Atlanta. She was the first white woman on the SNCC Executive Committee and remained in that position until 1964. Although Connie was a few years older than most of us, she connected very well with our vision and style of operating. Always there for our meetings, she gave insightful remarks without dominating our discussions and decision making. She encouraged us all to agree on a particular issue before we took action. Her presence alone was a great support for us and reassured us that we were doing the right thing. She was a constant reminder that we had strong allies outside of the Afro-American culture, that we were not alone in our struggle, and that the successful outcome of our cause would depend on winning the support of the majority of people. I've always been grateful for her wisdom and guidance, which helped to shape the way I work with people.

Another powerful protest that greatly affected me before coming to Selma was the 1955 Montgomery Bus Boycott, which targeted the public transportation system because of racial segregation. The boycott began when Rosa Parks was arrested for refusing to give up her bus seat to a white man. Dr. Martin Luther King Jr. was a young minister in town who became the leader of this protest and encouraged blacks to refuse to ride the buses. Because blacks were the majority of passengers on buses in Montgomery, when their business was withheld, the public transportation system was financially challenged. After 381 days of successful boycott of the buses (including a period of appeal to the Supreme Court), the Federal District Court declared that segregation on buses was unconstitutional. This was Dr. King's first successful campaign.

I recalled an earlier incident I had with my grandmother when the two of us got on the trolley car in Tampa. She deposited our coins in the receptacle in the front of the trolley but had to disembark and walk along the tracks to board in the back. Knowing that sometimes the conductor closed the door and drove away while we were walking to the rear door, we used to run back as quickly as we could. The conductor shut the door and began to pull away. My grandmother fell as I was reaching for the door. At age seven, I was helpless, too small to hold the door open and grab my grandmother at the same time. I felt like a sword cut me in half, and I vowed that I would do something about this problem one day. When I heard the bus boycott was successful in desegregating public transportation in Montgomery, I was elated that these problems could be solved. I was proud of the NAACP for waging the successful legal battle, and I was glad to be a youth member of this organization at age fifteen.

The first major change I recall was the landmark 1954 Supreme Court decision in *Brown v. Board of Education of Topeka, Kansas* that desegregated public schools. This ruled that the state laws requiring white and black students to attend separate public schools were unconstitutional.[9] By this time I had already gone to an integrated elementary school in

Philadelphia, from fourth through sixth grade, so this had a strong emotional impact on me. My principal was white and the faculty was integrated. I remember being appreciated as a human being there, and never experienced any form of disrespect because of my color. In fact, I was the commencement speaker for my sixth-grade graduation. "Living and Working Together" was the title of my speech. Integration was not just a thought in my mind, it was an experience I had. Having gone to a segregated school in first through third grade in Tampa, I knew the difference. I also knew that the difference in the color of my skin didn't make a difference in that integrated community. This experience had an influence on my determination to fight for change.

Even before my personal bus experience with Selma, I took a New Testament course with a white Southern Baptist professor at American Baptist Theological Seminary in Nashville, Rev. John Conley, who was from Selma. He had been a minister in Selma and coordinated the Vacation Bible Schools for both the white children and the black children at their various churches in town. One summer he decided to combine the final day picnic by having both groups meet together, as Christians, because they had that belief in common. The Southern Baptist Church got wind of this plan and stopped it. They were so upset that Rev. Conley would have suggested such an event that they told him, "If you like being around those people so much, then we'll send you to a place where you can be around them every day." So Rev. Conley was moved out of his position in Selma and sent to teach at an all-black college—American Baptist Theological Seminary. Although he was about as southern as he could get, with his slow, Alabama drawl, he was sincere, respectful, and dedicated to his students' learning. He never discussed racial issues in class, and I can't really describe him as liberal, but he was a person who viewed others as equals, even his students. Excited about teaching, he was even more enthused about our learning. His exams required intensive study, and he was proud when we excelled. He was a great example of how not all white people in Selma were racists. But he was also an illustration of how white people who favored integration or equal rights for black citizens were quickly shipped out of town. He was one of the people in the academic community who influenced my view of how people of other races could be supportive and helpful, and I came to look at him as an example of someone who took a stand based on his Christian convictions.

Dr. King reminded us that we had a responsibility to try to change the conditions that produced oppression and injustice, and he challenged us as individuals to take a firm stand. When I listened to Dr. King speak in public, it felt as if he were speaking directly to me. I felt personally connected and eager to do something. Whether by his speeches or conversing one-on-one, I always felt that his words were a personal assignment for me. From the first time I met him to the last words my friend and mentor spoke to me, I was always motivated to action, convinced that there was something I could do to make a difference.

Following the Albany, Georgia, movement in 1962, Dr. King had gone on a southern scouting mission, gathering information to make a decision about a location for a new campaign. Selma was one place he visited, and he spoke at a mass meeting there, filling the church. There was no police action in response to his speech, and it didn't create a stir in the white community because no one considered him a threat to their way of life at that time. Although some black leaders encouraged Dr. King to stay involved in Selma, he chose instead to initiate a campaign in Birmingham, Alabama. There were a few reasons for this decision. First, Selma was viewed as a quiet little town with not much controversy. His wife, Coretta, was from nearby Marion, along with Andrew Young's wife and Ralph Abernathy's wife, and those three civil rights leaders were familiar with the area on a personal level. Second, there was an oppressive feeling of fear in the community that kept black people from attempting to take any action that might upset the white citizens of Selma. There were no known acts of violence against blacks taking place in Dallas County that commanded national attention. Because of the overwhelming complacency of local blacks, Dr. King felt that the situation was not ripe for action at that point. Third, there was an oppressive white leadership in Birmingham, with Bull Connor as the commissioner of public safety. His widely known raging temper and reactionary responses to civil rights issues could possibly work in our favor. Fourth, there was already an SCLC stronghold in that community, with steadfast leader Rev. Fred Shuttlesworth working tirelessly there. His home had just been bombed for the third time. When Selma and Birmingham were compared for possibilities of a successful campaign, Birmingham came out on top. Birmingham was filled with more overt violence, already having experienced more than sixty bombings against blacks, suspected to have been carried out by the Ku Klux Klan. The needs in Birmingham seemed to be more pressing.

The first time I met Dr. King was when he came to Nashville in the spring of 1960 and spoke to us in the Fisk University gymnasium. It was an exciting moment to meet with him face-to-face. Although I had met many great leaders within the black community, such as the Howard University president Mordecai Johnson and the Morehouse College president Benjamin Mays, meeting Dr. King was akin to meeting the president of the United States. He was like our black president with the leadership he brought to the movement. I was on cloud nine. There was almost something spiritual about meeting him, like a divine presence. When I shook his hand the first time, I felt I was touching greatness.

Much of my reference to nonviolent action was based on Dr. King's Montgomery Bus Boycott strategies. I had consumed his book *Stride toward Freedom*. I had heard him speak on the radio, had read about him in the newspapers, and had seen him on television. When he came, he paid our SNCC group the highest compliment: "I've come to Nashville not to bring inspiration but to gain inspiration." I was very proud that he recognized the Nashville Student Movement and encouraged us.

The second time Dr. King and I met was that same spring in Raleigh, North Carolina, when SNCC was established. When I talked with Dr. King, I was always inspired by his words. I felt uplifted, buoyed by his presence. When the Nashville students and I arrived in Raleigh to join ranks with his organization, SCLC, I was bursting with youthful enthusiasm. We were also joined by some of our northern support groups with a mixture of white and black individuals, all committed to a common cause. There was electricity in the air, the desire to join with others who had been jailed or beaten. Such meetings reinforced the notion that we were not alone; this collection of college students was bonded by our experiences, dedication, and determination. We were partnering with prominent figures, such as Dr. King, James Farmer of CORE, James Lawson from the Nashville movement, prominent NAACP leaders, and others whom we had never met but knew by reputation. This was our first opportunity to share and compare strategies, and to create bonds that have lasted for more than fifty years.

My next encounter with Dr. King was the summer of 1960 at the Interracial Action Workshop sponsored by CORE in Miami, Florida, where I had a chance to spend more time with him, just the two of us, during poolside chats at the Sir John Hotel. Since I was a student at the American Baptist Theological Seminary, our conversations centered on the New Testament mandate that required Christians to love their enemy. We talked in depth about the meaning of love in the context of nonviolence. The other topic that engaged us was the concept of civil disobedience. As he talked, I came to have a clear and fuller understanding of how both love and civil disobedience could be applied on a practical level, not just in dialogical interaction. Afterward, a question that kept whirling around in my mind was "To what extent would having a leadership role in the movement affect my normal daily life?" Clearly, the commitment to civil rights and the devotion to family and children was a difficult balance for Dr. King.

Before I began my job in Selma, I needed advice from someone with practical experience in voter registration. I found the right man. When I left Tuskegee I went to Montgomery and met with Mr. Rufus Lewis, a funeral director and the former Alabama State University football coach. He had decades of experience working with voter registration founding citizenship schools in rural Alabama, and he laid out for me the strategy on how to accomplish this daunting task. A natural organizer, he had systematized neighborhoods in Montgomery block by block and appointed block captains to make sure everyone had information about voter registration. He held leadership roles in many black groups in Montgomery, including chair of the Voter Registration Committee and chair of the Transportation Committee, which coordinated travel during the Montgomery Bus Boycott. He was a member of Dexter Avenue Baptist Church, where Dr. King was pastor, and a founder of the Montgomery Improvement Association. For many years he worked closely with Dr. King. He shared his wisdom with me, instructing that we could register more voters by teaching people to fill out the application forms and take the literacy tests (a government practice used to judge the literacy of citizens and infamous as an unfair way to prohibit blacks from exercising their right to vote). The goal was to reach as many people as possible and prepare them to go to the county courthouse and register to vote. It was vital to support the local people in committing to this goal rather than having someone from the outside come in and tell them what to do. He advised me to identify a core group of black leaders and to train them so that they could, in turn, train and encourage people in their own community.

Mr. Lewis recommended that I visit the counties where the largest numbers of blacks lived so we would make the most difference in the marginal vote. In addition to Dallas County, we identified Wilcox, Lowndes, Marengo, and Perry Counties in central Alabama, where many blacks who had worked on plantations were now sharecroppers and still worked the land. These counties were part of what was called the "Black Belt," which included numerous counties across several southeastern states. It was originally named the Black Belt because the soil was dark and rich, which attracted many cotton plantation owners with slaves to settle there, eventually creating a predominantly black population. Over time, though, people began to associate the term Black Belt with this region because of the demographic reality of a heavy black population.

Mr. Lewis told me, "First, go by yourself to avoid drawing attention. Second, go quietly at night to visit people in their homes to lay a foundation of support instead of starting with a big church rally. Third, train a few people who are a little more educated. They can circulate around the neighborhoods in small groups and teach others to complete the forms." Mr. Lewis had learned that if people had practice completing the registration forms, it would give them confidence to attempt to register. Even if they didn't pass the test because it had been unfairly graded, they would at least know they had given it their best effort.

When I was working with Mr. Lewis it was like I was in class, being taught by a wise teacher. The challenge was going to be making it all happen. I had many mixed feelings. I was concerned that my actions might cause some repercussions that would put people who trusted me at risk. I was worried about the people I would work with, not wanting to jeopardize them or their families. Yet I was excited that I might have an impact on this Selma community and was eager to support and encourage them. I wanted to make them fully aware of what the consequences of their meetings might be, and I resolved that the choices made should be theirs, not mine. I wanted to give them the roadmap and let them walk toward change.

I had the advantage of having some experiences with my grandmother as she organized the church in Tampa where she held meetings at night in her home. I felt comfortable knowing this could work. Small gatherings presented an opportunity not only for people to learn about the voter registration application process and tests they would take, but also to give support to each other as people talked among themselves and bonded over a common cause. It seemed like a combination of missionary work and group therapy, helping people overcome their fears, take a stand, take a risk.

Mr. Lewis and I worked each morning, and then walked down the street to have lunch at Mrs. Annie Cooper's home. She was famous for her collard greens, cornbread, and sweet potato pie. Her delicious meals sustained me as we planned strategies for the most important project of my life, so far.

I knew right away that Selma was unique. There was a quiet stillness there, as if the town were enveloped in a shroud of fear. On my first day I noticed the various symbols of structural segregation. When I went into the barbershop on Main Street, I sat down and waited for a haircut. I looked at the black barbers, but the barbers never even glanced at me. They all busied themselves, cleaning their tools and brushes. I thought it was odd that they didn't speak to me or call me up for a cut, as there were no other customers in the shop. They simply wouldn't acknowledge me sitting there.

Finally, one barber mumbled, "We can't cut black hair."

"What?" I asked, puzzled. They were black barbers, but were they telling me that they would only cut hair for white men? Yes, that's exactly what they meant. So I got up and left, shaking my head in disbelief. I eventually found a barber in the community who cut hair for black men.

Another example of the blatant segregation here was the two-tiered sidewalks through the middle of town. Historically, blacks were expected to walk on the lower tier near the street, while whites walked on the upper tier. If a car, or years earlier a horse and buggy, splashed water or mud when it drove by, it would get people wet on the lower tier, not the upper tier. I had to learn where to walk in this town.

At the end of the month, I went into the bank to cash my check from SNCC, but the teller refused to cash it. It was a cashier's check for $1,000 that was to cover the costs of opening up the Selma office. I think they were suspicious that the check wasn't good since a black man was trying to cash it. They also knew I was with the Alabama Voter Registration Campaign and didn't want to help me at all. I insisted that they call the bank in Atlanta to verify its authenticity. It took me two more trips to the bank before they would finally cash it, and they certainly made it difficult for me. I had already been identified as an outsider coming into town to shake things up. I believe that the bank was hesitant to get involved or cooperate in any way with the voter registration drive.

There were several reasons why black people in this area were reluctant to register to vote. Their fear rose from the common knowledge about the fate of people who tried. I was told an account of one black man's experience. In adjacent Wilcox County years ago, a retired black minister had one wish in life—to vote. He walked into the courthouse to register, but the white registrar told him he couldn't register to vote because they weren't ready for that. He thanked them, put on his hat, and walked out. As he headed down the courthouse steps, he was shot and killed. This story and many others, passed down through the years, became folklore and only perpetuated the fear that attempting to register to vote was dangerous, and even life threatening.

Another chilling account known throughout Selma occurred during an earlier period when the minister at Brown Chapel African Methodist Episcopal (AME) Church, which we all called Brown Chapel, had mounted a protest demanding that the maids get paid one dollar a day. The minister got word from some maids who worked in the white homes that he was going to be attacked. The maids had overheard the wives discussing what was going to happen, apparently not thinking that blacks had ears. When a mob came to lynch him, it was expected, and the church officers hid him up in a loft of a church. The men of the church sneaked him out of town and he escaped.

Sadly, there was a consensus that if you stuck your neck out, you would get your head chopped off and there was no recourse; that if you took a stand against the system, it would only result in defeat. So why try? The more negative commentaries I heard about Selma, along with people's fears, the more I was inspired and determined to do something about it. I didn't know what to expect or what problems I might confront not only each day, but every night. It was a twenty-four-hour tension because it was common knowledge that the suffering often came at night with bombs or shootings. I slept only about two hours at a time, awaking at any small sound. My body was conditioned to be aware of every noise. Even to this day I sleep lightly after years of deliberate practice. It's a stress that has never left.

Both Gandhi and Dr. King called for specificity of goals in a movement to provide clarity and concreteness. The goals of this Voter Registration Campaign were twofold: first, to implement nonviolent direct action to increase the number of black people being able to exercise their voice in government, which was their right as American citizens; second, to help build a case for the federal government to prove that the county governments were discriminating against black voter registrants. The U.S. Department of Justice had already issued injunctions, which prevented anyone from interfering with citizens who were attempting to register to vote. They had filed suits in several counties, charging people who were harassing those who tried to register to vote. My job was to aid the applicants and to encourage large numbers of citizens to attempt to register. If people didn't attempt to vote, there was no proof of discrimination.

To help reach these goals, I broke the tasks down into smaller units. The first strategy was to identify a group of black citizens committed to the cause who would be willing to work within their community. We needed to organize voter registration classes where potential voters could get assistance on filling out the application form and learning how to pass the literacy tests. Second, we planned to have weekly mass meetings at a later time that would serve to educate, inform, and motivate the people. Third, we wanted to arrange for large numbers of blacks to attempt to register to vote at the county courthouses on the two days a month that the voter registration offices were open. I knew that these tasks wouldn't be easy, but I was ready to try.

2

Shackles of Fear, Handcuffs of Hopelessness

Almost always, the creative, dedicated minority has made the world better.

—Dr. Martin Luther King Jr.

It was a cold January morning in 1963 when I first drove into Selma to start the project, and in less than fifteen minutes a police car was following my automobile, and I was driving only in the black community. I concluded there had to be someone in the neighborhood who tipped off the police that a stranger was in town. It was disheartening to realize that blacks were turning against each other. One of the fears expressed more than once was that "these Freedom Riders will come down here and get your children thrown in jail, with no money to get them out." However, rather than doubts and fears looming large in my mind on hearing these stories, I became more curious as to how this community got that way. I was eager to talk with people, particularly older people, to learn about the experiences that shaped their way of thinking.

In the fall of 1962 I had just married Colia Liddell in Nashville, and my wife accompanied me to Selma. Many of us in the movement married young because we didn't know how long we'd survive. We were both twenty-two years old, just kids really. I first met Colia on the Freedom Rides a year earlier in Jackson, Mississippi. She went to Tougaloo College, a private school near Jackson, and was extremely bright and courageous. Colia and I first lived at the home of Mrs. Amelia Boynton, a strong leader in the black community and the person who initially invited SNCC to come to Selma. She gave me valuable insight into the inner workings of the Selma community. I'm proud to say that she has been a lifelong friend.

Then we moved in with a schoolteacher, Mrs. Margaret Moore, and her family until an apartment became available. Mrs. Moore was a master's-level teacher and had lived in Selma for many years. She owned rental property and graciously opened her home to us. I enjoyed her superb cooking, as well as her intelligent conversation and insightful thinking. As a by-product of my new living arrangement I became concerned about her safety and her involvement in the movement. Because I was there to mount the Voter Registration Campaign, this generated hostile feelings on the part of many whites. But not once did she show fear or discomfort. In her face could be seen quiet courage, with confidence and assuredness for her mission. Her pursuit of justice and equality was fact. She had a clear expectation that the voting campaign would succeed. She was there and ready wherever and whenever she was needed. Self-assured, posture erect, chin up and shoulders back, Mrs. Moore seemed almost to strut when she walked. She was an avid participant in marches and demonstrations. In later years Mrs. Moore was often referred to as an "invisible giant" because of her continued efforts and behind-the-scenes work to improve life for black people. Her children—a young son, Reginald, and two teenage daughters, Harriet and Gwen—were well mannered and well disciplined, not because she was stern and rigid, but rather because she expected them to act with intelligence and to use good judgment. And they did. Mrs. Moore taught them early on a life's lesson of standing up for what they believed. She was a stranger to fear and had a passion for service and community. As a teacher she went beyond the call of duty, often teaching students after school about their real black history, not what white people had written in the history books. She not only was well acquainted with her subject matter but also showed enormous love and compassion for her students.

Our SNCC workers mostly came from big cities and college towns. Frank Holloway from Atlanta joined me for a short while to help me get set up in the office, but he didn't stay very long. Some workers put on bib overalls to dress like farmers and people in the community, to blend in and relate to the local people. To get to know the people of Selma, I visited with them on their front porches, as I did with the retired postal worker Mr. Robert Reagon. He told me, "I've lived here all my life. I've traveled all around the world and know for certain that there is no place on earth as bad as Selma, Alabama. Son, I hate to tell you, but you are wasting your time, you won't accomplish anything here. I'd like to help you, but my hands is tied." He was not the only one to tell me this.

When I was on a plane flying from Atlanta headed to Montgomery, another passenger heard me talking about my job, turned around, and said, "You must be desperate if you're going to take a job in Selma." Even complete strangers were warning me that Selma was an undesirable place to live.

As I heard these stories I began to see clearly why the other SNCC workers who had come to Selma concluded that nothing could be done. After being there a while, I sensed that the concern of many of the black people was not only for themselves; they were equally afraid for my safety. Individuals I had met in private avoided me in public, fearing that associating with me would put their families and themselves in jeopardy. People driving down the street would not wave or even make eye contact. I noticed people crossing the street or turning to walk in another direction so they wouldn't have to pass me or greet me. I could see them physically draw up when I'd approach. Fear caused their shoulders to rise and stiffen, as they'd quietly but swiftly move away from me. It was a lonely, isolated time.

It was easy to see that some people were uncomfortable in my presence, and it made me feel at times that I was imposing on them. Connecting with me was jeopardizing their relationships with well-established contacts they had spent years developing. It was like these people were imprisoned behind cold walls, and I could feel the chill. But at the same time, because of the close, warm relationship I had with a few key people, I was able to fight against that icy barrier that had encaged their emotions. I understood that they didn't feel free but had become accustomed to a hopeless existence. When the SNCC leaders had said nothing could happen here, their words were truer than I ever imagined. Yet I still rejected that notion. I struggled to put myself in the position of someone constrained by the shackles of fear and the handcuffs of hopelessness. What did Selma men mean when they told me, "I'd like to help you, son, but my hands is tied"?

Soon after I arrived in Selma I went straight to the sheriff's office to inform him I was in town, showing him respect. The sheriff at the time was the notorious Jim Clark, who was a staunch segregationist and greatly feared by most black persons in the community. He was infamous for his abuse of blacks. His physical presence was daunting. He was a stocky man with a solid build and a swagger to his walk, his gun always visible. A stern look formed a permanent scowl on his face. Everything about this man spoke to an inevitable war he was waging. He wore a military-style uniform, complete with a helmet or military hat, as though he were in an army. There was no doubt about who was in charge in this office.

It was not uncommon in the rural areas of the South where there were large populations of blacks for sheriffs to play a major role in maintaining and enforcing segregation in a style reminiscent of the Old West. In some areas there was no chief of police, so the sheriff ruled. He had a large territory to control, and understandably his reputation played a significant role in maintaining control. Jim Clark abused his power as sheriff to make examples out of people so that his reputation would spread and no one would mess with him. He sported a reputation of taking action toward any deviant behavior, and his posse was tantamount to a legalized, state-sponsored lynch mob.

I reported to the sheriff's office for three reasons. First, I wanted to establish an official relationship. Even though I was a SNCC worker, my task was an official project of the SRC, an organization that was formed to collect facts regarding racial problems in the southern states. This group was pivotal in backing state committees because it encouraged people to become involved in their local communities. Second, I wanted him to understand that I was not trying to sneak and hide from the law, or slip and slide around the community. I wanted to impress on him that I was not afraid, and that it would be useless to try to intimidate me. He didn't have to come looking for me; I was right here in plain sight. Third, I needed to know what he looked like. I was curious about how he would respond to me, face-to-face. I was well aware of Sheriff Clark's reputation as mean spirited and short tempered. Even the hat cocked sideways on his head reflected his cocky attitude. It was apparent that he was used to going out looking for blacks rather than having a black man come looking for him.

When the sheriff looked into my eyes, he saw no fear, and he looked away, making little eye contact when he talked. Sheriff Clark may not have seen fear in my eyes, but it was there inside me. Because of his reputation I knew I needed to make a strong statement, so I suppressed my fear; I stomped on it. I had already anticipated the many things that could happen—he could punch me, shove me, beat me, arrest me, shoot me. Honestly, I'm still surprised that these things didn't happen. I was a skinny little guy, only five feet nine inches tall, with a twenty-six-inch waist and weighing 126 pounds. I certainly didn't threaten him physically. I mustered up the courage, then felt a calmness settle over my body. No, he saw no fear when he glared at me, but it was there, just invisible.

I told him where I lived so if he needed to get in touch he knew how to contact me. I even asked how I could get in touch with him. He told me, "If you want to talk to me you can reach me here at the office." I asked him about after hours, and he said, "Just call here." I first thought that he was putting me off, but I found out later that he often spent the night at the jail, so that really was the best place to reach him. Surprisingly, I found it wouldn't be hard for anyone to find me as my address was listed on the front page of the *Selma Times Journal*.

I was well aware that to be effective in bringing about positive change in a community, I needed to garner support from the constituencies in various organizations. These included churches, educational institutions, teacher unions, and civic clubs. I further identified pastors, principals, teachers, business professionals, and club leaders. It was my job to mobilize these community leaders into skilled organizers so that their groups and organizations would follow them. I came to understand that although there were independent professionals in the black Selma community, they were mostly an oppressed group who had concluded, not only out of fear but also out of hopelessness, that it was not a good idea to challenge the system. They felt it was a waste of time and energy to try to change things. So to keep peace and order, they stayed in their place and didn't rock the boat.

I met an eighty-nine-year-old minister who recognized that I was a young minister advocating change and told me, "I can get anything I want from white people, you just have to know how to do it. Here's what I do." Then he knelt down on one knee, grabbed his hat, and held it in his hands against his chest subserviently, eyes to the ground. Whew! If he was an example of black leadership in this community, I knew I had my work cut out for me.

While the fear of the majority of blacks was so thick you could feel it in the air, there was a group of black men and women in Selma who were strong and committed. They were not dependent on white hiring and were willing to take risks in the Voter Registration Campaign. These few key people were independent, not just economically: they had the unusual courage to stand up for their beliefs. Many of these men and women had lived in the Selma community for a number of years and had a sense of history. Some had served their country in the military. From their experiences growing up and from the support of their families they had developed a sense of self-worth and formed strong values. It's one thing to get registered to vote individually, but it's another thing to say *we*, as a community, need to have *all* citizens registered to vote. Massive votes had more impact than a few single votes. Most of these black leaders recognized that it was not enough to participate in the system as an individual; they had to be part of a group to have influence. The Dallas County Voters League became the avenue of change. What members of this group had in common was that they wanted to have influence and make changes. By coming together they reinforced each other and became examples for others to emulate. Since the Voter Registration Campaign was going to be a statewide campaign, it was critical to identify people who lived in Dallas County, who were familiar with this kind of work, and who supported it. We needed to demonstrate that it was possible to get a large number of people registered in Dallas County to be an example for other counties in the state. This became the primary strategy group. Even though our adversaries threatened us, we stood firm.

The two people who affected my life the most during my time in Selma were Mrs. Amelia Boynton and her husband, Samuel. Mrs. Boynton was an active member of the NAACP, and with her husband and six others, she founded the Dallas County Voters League. Before the formation of the Dallas County Voters League, a black veteran of three wars, Mr. C. J. Adams, had founded the Selma Civics Voter League. Mr. Adams spent a great deal of time assisting other black veterans in Selma by helping them fill out the proper forms to apply for their benefits from the Veterans Administration. The white authorities in Selma opposed his activities to such an extent that his life was threatened, he was jailed several times, and he was even forced to leave the city.[1]

The Boyntons owned an insurance company, an employment agency, and a real estate business within the black community. Having graduated from the Tuskegee Institute in 1927, Mrs. Boynton was well educated in school and in life. She was always there to bail me out of jail, when necessary. Mrs. Boynton was born in Savannah, Georgia, and her first experiences involving human rights began when she worked for women's suffrage in her early years. She was acquainted with George Washington Carver at the Tuskegee Institute, and he became an influence on her life.

Mrs. Boynton stood tall and regal with a perpetual smile yet a manner of quiet defiance. She held high principles and had a long arm reach into the community. But her heart reached even further. With a keen mind given to profound analysis of issues and problems, she believed in taking action. Generous to a fault, she shared her time and resources with people, especially those who were most needy. Her courage was incomparable. She stood face-to-face and toe-to-toe with Sheriff Jim Clark many times. Eager to see change and progress in Selma, she worked for improving life for all black people. Mrs. Boynton was an independent thinker and an eternal optimist. When others didn't dare to hope, she had hope. When we experienced setbacks, she saw progress and movement toward our goal, recognizing that setbacks were preludes to comebacks. Her ever-strong will, fighting spirit, and determination gave me inspiration and confidence that the people in Selma could change.

Mrs. Boynton frequently said, "People need to learn how to stand up for their rights. No one's going to give you anything, you must demand it." That sentiment carried over not only into voter registration but into all aspects of life. She believed that people should be independent and request an action by standing up with confidence, never cowering or begging, weak and helpless. She said, "Nonviolence has power." She lived it and was a model for me and for others.

Today I am still close with Mrs. Boynton, who is more than one hundred years old and still has her sharp wit and gentle nature. She can recall names of people involved in the movement during this period that I have long forgotten. She continues to speak to groups of people who come to Selma to study the civil rights movement and tells her story to hushed and enthralled audiences. As seasoned as she is, her voice is strong and her stories carry power and emotion. Mrs. Boynton and I were so bound together in our faith and in the movement that our fate was intertwined. She's an amazing woman whom I am honored to know and love.

Although Mr. Boynton was in failing health when I met him, and living in a nursing home, people described him as a mild-mannered man who had a serious focus and a keen sense for business opportunities. He knew how to "turn a dollar." He had a passion for justice and was an advocate for improving the conditions of blacks, and he helped bring economic stability to the community. A graduate of the Tuskegee Institute in the class of 1925, he always placed a strong emphasis on education and guided people to opportunities to improve their conditions. Because of his earnest will and his success in business, he was well respected and admired in both the black and white populations. Even though some whites didn't like his activity with voter registration, they were comfortable with his insurance and real estate interests. When property sold, people built houses, which benefited many businesses, including those of whites. Mr. Boynton was a farm agent for that area of Alabama, responsible for assisting the farmers with the crops, purchasing equipment, and connecting them with resources from the federal government. He encouraged them to register to vote and to participate in government. He and his wife were among the few black entrepreneurs in Selma.

I used to relieve Mrs. Boynton and sit with her husband at night in the nursing home, just so that if there was a problem, someone would be there. Even in the nursing home, as sick as he was, he would call out as someone passed his room and ask, "Have you registered to vote yet?" He was noted for saying, "A voteless people is a hopeless people." He was recruiting even on his deathbed and literally, with his very last breath, hopeful until the very end. In a mysterious way I felt some transference of mission by just being beside Mr. Boynton, even though I had never actually talked with him since he had been too ill. His life's work was my life's work, and I felt privileged to be in the presence of someone who had made such noble contributions to the cause of civil rights. When Mr. Boynton passed away, he had devoted an entire life of service to the black community.

Many young people said to me that they would like to get involved with the Dallas County Voters League but that the leadership wasn't providing direction. The president was still Mr. Boynton, even though he had been too ill to lead the organization for quite some time. Nobody had been appointed in his place because the group didn't want to be disrespectful of him. I assured them that Mr. Boynton wouldn't mind. I realized that these were just excuses, though, because the real reason for the group's paralysis was simply that they didn't know what to do.

The Boyntons' son, Bruce, a graduate of Howard University Law School, continued his parents' cause. Bruce grew up in a household that was focused on justice. He learned at an early age to stand up for what is right and to work hard to make life better for black people. Bruce was the Boynton in the U.S. Supreme Court case of *Boynton v. Virginia*, which dealt with the interstate commerce laws and segregation of public facilities on interstate highways. Because of this winning case, the Freedom Riders of 1961 had the legal foundation to challenge southern practices and gained courage to challenge the law.[2]

I went to Selma fully aware of the risks involved. However, I focused my efforts on the tremendous impact the campaign would have if it succeeded. I was very proud to be a part of this challenge. Looking back, it was only because of the small group of black supporters that the campaign was able to accomplish its mission. They had courage in spite of knowing what could and did happen to others who had taken stands, from loss of jobs to beatings, jailing, and even death. Reprisal was frequently exercised against family members of those who stood up. Black women and men had learned to survive within the system, not making any waves or stirring up trouble, simply living by avoiding violence. This is called "negative peace."

It was understandable that so many people had feelings of trepidation and the strong belief that you couldn't get anything done in Selma. Those comments only made me more determined. The naysayers might be right, but I had to try to make changes myself. I believed that it was possible based on the previous experiences I'd had applying nonviolence as a strategy in a number of other campaigns. Selma appeared to be more difficult, but I felt this was only because nonviolent direct action had not yet been attempted. Even though I found myself surrounded by a community of doubt, I knew nothing would happen unless I tried. I wanted to move this town toward "positive peace," creating a social system that would serve the needs of the entire community and developing constructive resolutions to conflict. I've never claimed that practicing peace was easy, and it sure wasn't going to be easy in Selma, Alabama.

I believed in cultivating a climate for change by building a solid foundation within the existing structure of a community. My goal was to support local leadership, as opposed to rolling into town and creating a separate organization. This was a slow, methodical approach that I had learned from my grandmother. I knew I needed to connect with a local organization, so I considered my best options. One group was the "Twelve High," a club of twelve men whose stated mission was to get high on Friday night and stay high until Monday morning. Another group was the Dallas County Voters League, dedicated to promoting voter registration for blacks. There wasn't much question about which group to align with.

Rather than opening a new SNCC office, I assigned myself to become the staff person for the Dallas County Voters League, so I would have a local community identity and try to resuscitate the organization. Mrs. Boynton offered me space in her real estate office, which was already shared with Attorney J. L. Chestnut. Even though the Dallas County Voters League met only once a year to determine who they would vote for, Mrs. Boynton called a special meeting to discuss ways to expand our efforts and get more people involved in the voter registration effort.

I met once a week to plan strategy with a group of eight community leaders from the Dallas County Voters League—Mrs. Boynton, Mrs. Marie Foster, Rev. Frederick Reese, Mr. James E. Gildersleeve, Mr. Ulysses Blackmon, Mr. Ernest Doyle, Rev. J. D. Hunter Sr., and Rev. H. Shannon. I was glad to be able to report my activities to this local ad hoc group. We would receive a report on how many people had registered to vote on the prescribed registration days, which were only twice a month. We organized the mass meetings and decided where we would have them, who would speak, and how to promote the voter education workshops to maximize attendance.

One night there was a real test of courage on the part of a few of us who held regular meetings at Mrs. Boynton's office. A rumor had circulated that if we were caught in this meeting the law officials were going to raid the office and arrest us for plotting, planning, and engaging in unlawful activity. Mrs. Boynton's office was right across the street from the police station, literally a stone's throw away. We always suspected that we were being observed from an upstairs window that looked directly across at her office. On the night when we had our planning meeting there was a question as to who would show up in spite of that impending threat. We referred to this as the "I ain't scared" meeting. One by one, each person showed up, the original "Courageous Eight," as we lovingly called ourselves, although some people referred to us as the "Crazy Eight." We had our meeting and were on edge in anticipation of an assault, but nothing happened. It was either a false rumor or the authorities changed their minds. Possibly it was an attempt to see if a rumor could scare us out of meeting. It didn't.

There had been several small meetings for adults about the problems with voter registration, organized by the Boyntons. However, Mrs. Boynton attributes the true success of the mass meetings to engaging the youth to join the movement. I felt that it was important to involve the young people in the voter registration process, even though they weren't yet voting age. They needed to realize the significance of the vote and to see the registration process as it was and how they could help change it. They could participate in other important ways, as they learned about the voter registration process. They were old enough to have some influence on their parents by encouraging them to register to vote. Mahatma Gandhi said, "You must be the change you want to see in the world." I believe that the youth of Selma wanted to be a part of the change that they saw coming. Even children in elementary school became involved, children such as Sheyann Webb and Joanne Blackmon (Bland).

Throughout the summer students engaged in voter registration efforts in a number of ways. They observed the process of registering, talked to adults about voting, attended mass meetings, recruited adults to come to classes, and distributed flyers to publicize various events. The youth gained experience by observing the people who were lined up to register. They noted who was there and kept records of those who attempted to register. Some people wanted to register anonymously and, out of embarrassment, wouldn't report to us if they had been denied, but they were victims of blatant discrimination. One way the system suppressed voter participation was to effectively keep people registering as individuals, not as groups. Some people thought they'd be victimized if they identified with a group, and preferred to remain autonomous so they could quietly obtain their rights rather than depending on group pressure demanding their rights. They might have thought, "I'm not a part of a mass group. I'm doing this individually." I viewed the situation from a systemic perspective. The reason we had to keep count was to have a more accurate record of the number of people who had attempted to register so we could record those who were refused.

One of the most effective training methods we used was role-playing to simulate the experiences the registrants or the youth might encounter, preparing them to face the violence, beatings, and arrests. We instructed them how they should behave and respond. For example, some young people would form a circle and others would be on the inside. The outside group yelled insults, called names, and pushed the group in the middle, just as it might happen, and had happened to many of us in past protests. We couldn't simulate the dangerous situations of actual beatings, but we could pretend to be policemen yelling and shoving. We trained them to not say anything because sometimes it's hard to control what we say. We had learned over time that people's behavior is often a reaction to what they hear more than to what they see. Their emotions are often elevated by words and sounds. This is why we practiced reacting nonviolently to name calling and shouting.

Another strategy we found effective in training the young people focused on keeping a positive attitude when they were arrested. They needed to learn how to avoid violence and to cooperate by responding to reasonable requests. We emphasized the value of not resisting or showing negative attitudes toward the jailers, as one goal was to win the jailers over. We encouraged them to sing to lift their spirits and give motivation and inspiration to each other. Singing about freedom would keep them feeling hopeful and strong in unity with each other. They were not there alone. I hoped they could show a bombardment of courage rather than the silence of fear.

The Birmingham movement was going on at the same time I was in Selma. I regularly traveled ninety miles up to Birmingham to help train the youth there in a similar way that I had been trained in Nashville. While Rev. Jim Lawson was at Vanderbilt University's Divinity School he began a series of nonviolence training workshops for students at surrounding colleges. Rev. Lawson, who became my mentor, convinced me that the most important area of work for me and the nonviolence movement for social change was the training for education and leadership. The work he did in the training became a model for me. As I look back, I realize that his impact was felt in every successful campaign that occurred in the 1960s because so many civil rights leaders were trained by Jim Lawson.

Jim helped me understand the strength of suffering. Numerous times I heard him echo, "Honor and suffering are redemptive." I constantly sought that. I tried to experiment with his teachings in the street. It's one thing to accept the teachings intellectually in the classroom, but it's much more difficult to live the teachings in your actions in the midst of a clash when blood is being spilt. This was the real test of his words. He talked a lot about love, asking, "Can you truly love those who abuse you, in a humanistic way?" I wasn't sure. I kept thinking, "What good would it do to love them?" I found that those workshops strengthened my own character. Lawson's teachings presented an alternative response to our opponents.

Although the Birmingham movement was focused on the equalization of public accommodations, whereas Selma concentrated on voting rights, the process for training in nonviolent direct action was the same. The workshops instructed high school students who were enthusiastic and ready to put their training into action. Jim Bevel and his wife, Diane Nash Bevel, were two of the leaders of the Birmingham movement, and we had been close friends for years. We often shared our time supporting each other, but I didn't participate in the demonstrations there in Birmingham, as I couldn't risk arrest.

Jim Bevel and I had been college roommates and close colleagues in Nashville, where we learned together about nonviolent direct action from Rev. Lawson's workshops. Where there needed to be action, Bevel was always there at the forefront. He was involved with SNCC, SCLC, the Nashville sit-ins, the Freedom Rides, and the Mississippi Voting Rights Movement, and now was active in Birmingham. He was unwavering in his commitment to the civil rights movement, and Dr. King respected him as a key strategist.

Analytical and persuasive, Diane Nash had been the articulate spokesperson for our Nashville movement and the superb coordinator for the Nashville contingency for Freedom Rides, always able to convey a sense of urgency. Wherever there was a campaign for civil rights, Diane was right there in the middle of it, planning and organizing.

When Diane and Jim got married it was a bonding of brains and spirit, with both sharing a passion for social change and for helping others. When some of us SNCC workers were raising bond money to bail three fellow activists out of jail in Louisiana, Diane was in jail in Jackson, Mississippi, arrested for refusing to move to the side of the courtroom reserved for blacks. Even though she was nearly nine months pregnant, she refused bond, saying, "Any negro child born anywhere in Mississippi is born in jail."

At SNCC we were all concerned about her child being born in jail, so we strategized how to get her to leave. There was no coercing her, so my thought was, "What would make her *want* to get out of jail?" Knowing her kind heart, I felt that she would put the needs of others above her own, so I proposed that we ask her to speak at a mass meeting to raise funds to get the three workers released from jail. Diane's father was a prominent dentist in Detroit, and if we could convince her to speak at a meeting in that city, it would be a big draw. It worked. She left jail, flew to Detroit, and spoke at the meeting at the Bethel AME Church, pastored by Rev. Joseph L. Roberts. Two days later she gave birth to a baby girl, Sherri, in Albany, Georgia. Although Diane had fervent personal convictions, her love and concern for other people was overriding.

Each movement feeds on the previous movement and gives impetus to the next one. The Selma youth were inspired by the Birmingham youth. If any movement had the image of massive youth participation (younger than college age), it would be Birmingham, often referred to as the Children's Movement.

The Selma youth's enthusiasm, passion, and excitement were spurred on by watching the events in Birmingham unfold in May 1963. They were moved by the four thousand young people who left school to march, in spite of being attacked by ferocious dogs, being sprayed by water hoses, and being locked in jail. In fact, some of those Birmingham adolescents I trained in direct action came as volunteers to work with the youth in Selma. That summer when they got out of school, two dynamic student leaders, Alexander Brown and Ronnie Howard, came to Selma to help me with organizing the youth and conducting workshops.

Deeply affected by the Montgomery Bus Boycott back in 1955, Alex had become wholeheartedly involved in civil rights, and he joined the Birmingham NAACP Youth Council at age thirteen. Alex told me that Dr. King's message of love for all of God's children had deeply resonated with him. When the word spread that Dr. King was coming to town to lead the campaign, Alex thought it was the happiest day of his life. Alex had been arrested and was in the Birmingham Jail at the same time Dr. King was imprisoned and wrote his famous "Letter from the Birmingham Jail." Inspired by his time with Dr. King, Alex had emerged from jail a solid student leader.

These young men were in the best position to share not only what they had been taught but also their own personal experiences of demonstrations, arrests, jail, and beatings. The young people in Selma listened to every word, riveted. Youth inspired youth.

Most of these workshops took place at the St. Elizabeth's Mission Catholic Church, led by Father Maurice Ouellet, who made the facility available to the young people. The trainings encompassed a two-part process—understanding and practice. The training focused on understanding the philosophy of nonviolence and why it is much more powerful than violence. We helped the participants grasp the idea that when they are nonviolent, they maintain control over their interactions, as opposed to losing their temper and thus losing the battle. If one loses self-control, one is already defeated.

It was necessary for the youth to comprehend why people were violent toward them. If adversaries were able to provoke a violent reaction, it would result in more violence. If they responded in a nonviolent way, the opponent would be defeated, having failed to incite them to violence. The youth learned over time that they held valuable internal resources that were stronger than external physical weapons. Violence perpetrated on them would empower them rather than defeat them.

The trainings focused not only on being able to restrain oneself but on being able to transform natural fear and anger into positive responses. We taught them to look the adversary in the eye and let the offender peer directly into our souls. For example, when someone is attacking them, and shouting at them, could they think, "But I love you" in a humanistic way? It's much more difficult than fighting back physically.

We wanted students to realize that although opponents may be behaving violently at a particular moment, deep within them is the capacity to act more humanely. We want to allow the real essence of who they are as human beings to emerge. The training gave students practical experience of fighting back with love, striking the person's conscience rather than their body. As long as they could control themselves, they had the possibility to control the situation. Unusual but genuine behavior has the potential to arrest the conscience of the assailant.

The advantage of working with youth is that they get excited by new ideas, experiences, drama, playacting, and games. But when they participate in a demonstration, it's real, not a simulation. Then it becomes a test, a reality test. It's not how well they did in their training, but how well they could perform in the real world.

Creativity and the arts were taught in the trainings, for activists often need to think and act creatively in uncertain situations. Because music is a powerful tool, we practiced rewriting lyrics to well-known songs to fit the movement. Growing up singing in the church choir I always loved music, and adding verses to traditional songs, such as "Keep Your Eyes on the Prize," was fun and meaningful.

> Come on people, don't be slow
> Selma Alabama is next to go.
> Hold on, hold on,
> Keep your eyes on the prize, hold on.
> I don't know the song but I know the note
> They're marching in Selma for the right to vote.
> Hold on, hold on,
> Keep your eyes on the prize, hold on.
> Some say fast, some say slow,
> We all say Jim Crow's got to go.
> Hold on, hold on,
> Keep your eyes on the prize, hold on.
> We had our ups and we had our downs,
> But we made up our minds we wouldn't turn around.
> Hold on, hold on,
> Keep your eyes on the prize, hold on.

The young people bring the future to the movement. We know about the past atrocities and disappointments. We know the tragic acts of violence that have happened. But when I see the spirited young people becoming involved, I envision a bright future, a hope and a promise of better times to come.

One day I sent some high school students over to the courthouse to observe who was there and to record who had or had not been successful in registering, a simple but helpful task for youth. Selma was such a close-knit town that the local students knew almost everyone who was there. However, Sheriff Clark came out of his office and chased them off, and he even arrested one of the young men who was just standing in the hall-way. Even though the young man wasn't breaking any law, Sheriff Clark said he had no business in the courthouse and arrested him for vagrancy.

Alex Brown burst into our office with Olympic strides, eyes bugged out, terrified. He was running so fast that he had to grab hold of the doorframe to stop. He shouted, "Sheriff Clark, he's after us! He grabbed Boise Reese and threw him in jail, and he's gonna get the rest of us!"

Calmly, I got up. "Come on. Let's go back to Jim Clark's office."

He cried, "We can't go back there, he'll arrest us too!" I didn't want him running from the sheriff. He needed to develop some courage and self-confidence.

I walked back downtown with him to the sheriff's office, a few blocks away. He was walking several paces behind me, so he'd have running room. In fact, he even had one foot turned ready to fly. He must have thought that his freedom was connected to the speed of his feet. We approached the long counter in the sheriff's office with the secretary sitting behind it.

I said, "I'd like to see Sheriff Clark. Tell him Rev. LaFayette is out here to see him." Clark sauntered out with his hat cocked sideways. I was calm but firm, and demanded, "Where's Boise Reese? I understand you have him, and I want him—now!"

Clark said, "He's not here. He's over at the city jail."

I glared at him, not really sure if I believed him. There was a holding cell downstairs where they kept people ready to transfer over to the county jail, and I thought he might be there. "Call over there," I said. "I want to make bond for him."

He said, "You've got to go over there yourself." He glanced over at the door toward Alex and said, "Hey, who you got over there with you?" I turned around and all I could see was the back of Alex running full speed down the sidewalk.

I said, "I don't see anybody," then walked out.

When the sheriff asked the students to leave the courthouse, Boise evidently didn't get out of there fast enough. He was the first person arrested in the campaign. When I asked at the jail why he had been arrested, nobody would tell me anything. Attorney Chestnut became involved, and Boise was eventually released. My concern was the physical harm that might come to him out of the sight of the public and the media. The jailors could have accused him of resisting arrest, and no telling what could have happened.

The lesson in bravery took a little longer for Alex to learn. The only way he could learn courage was by facing Jim Clark, not avoiding him. It was an important experience for him to begin to overcome his fear of Sheriff Clark. I knew that if he were ever to become a leader, he had to control his emotions. Eventually, he did.

I reversed the way to think about Jim Clark, emphasizing this point: "The sheriff is not after you; you are after the sheriff." The way Alex was running that day, I don't think he quite believed that statement. In most of the Alabama counties the sheriff was elected by the people, and since we were getting involved with voter registration, the sheriff's position was in jeopardy. The sheriff held the billy club, but the people held the ballot. Alex's fear gave me even more courage, because I saw what being afraid could do, and it was ugly. We had to set the examples, not just talk and lecture, but model expected behavior so the youth could grow into strong individuals. In moments of crisis, significant lessons are learned.

In time, Alex began to set examples for other young people. Fear develops from the unknown. People have knowledge of what has happened to others and they become uncertain about what will happen to them in similar situations. In most cases people tried desperately to avoid danger. By returning to the scene that terrified him, Alex was gradually able to build up the strength to resist trepidation. Each step he took back to the sheriff's office moved him closer to courage and further from fear. There was always the impulse to flee, to escape negative conditions through flight rather than fight. The emotional force and adrenalin surge that come over people when they're afraid can empower them to override their physical limitations.

One indication that the movement is in the people is when they sing their own protest songs. Three little girls, Germaine Platts, age fourteen, Sharon Platts, age twelve, and Arleen Ezell, age fourteen, wrote and sang the first freedom song of Selma, that I know of. This song inspired the entire black community and poured strength into everyone's hearts with the children's deeply felt sincerity.

Freedom is a comin' and it won't be long
Freedom is a comin' and we're marching on
And if you want to be free, come and go with me.

We are marching on to freedom land
So come along and join, hand in hand
Striving on and singing a song
I hope we're not alone.

We are fighting for our equal rights,
So come on and join hands and fight
Striving on and singing a song
I know we're not alone.

Joan Baez came to Selma for a few days to support the cause. She met the three girls and was impressed with their singing and earnestness in writing a song for the movement. One morning Joan sat on the steps of the Tabernacle Baptist Church with the three girls, strumming her guitar, and sang "This Little Light of Mine." I was assured that I had come to the right city when those sweet voices carried through the town with strength and honesty. The movement was in these three little girls, and we were ready to put the movement into the rest of Selma. Even though they were young, they were willing and committed. Singing is a form of protest, but more than that, the songs were a healing process for all of us.

3

Preparing to Register to Vote

> Freedom and justice cannot be parceled out in pieces to suit political convenience. I don't believe you can stand for freedom for one group of people and deny it to others.
>
> —Coretta Scott King

The voter registration office at the Dallas County Courthouse was open only two days a month, the first and third Thursdays, so this limited the opportunities to attempt to register. When I heard about this ridiculous twice-a-month schedule, I thought, "Well, we're going to change that!" Some weeks people gathered at Brown Chapel and marched to the voter registration office together. They would line up waiting to register, calling attention to the issue of voter registration, which was part of the direct action strategy. The registrars were known to open the office late and move through the process so slowly that few registrants had the chance to register.

A written examination, which was referred to as the literacy test (see appendix A for an example), was given to every person who registered to vote. It was called a literacy test by the people who were taking it. The registrar called it an application. This was another way of discriminating against black people: using the results of this test to deny them the right to vote. Historically, a form of literacy test had been used to disqualify African Americans from voting following the Reconstruction era in the late 1800s because of white southerners' fear of black domination. Literacy tests were also used in 1917 as a component of the immigration process, then continued in the southern states with the voter registration process.[1]

The language of the literacy test was difficult and confusing, and often went over the heads of uneducated registrants. They could barely read the words on the test, much less understand what it was asking. It's one thing to determine whether a person is literate, and another thing for them to understand the information required on the test. Words such as "impeachment" and "reconsideration" interfered with their comprehension of the questions and hindered them from answering correctly. My favorite absurd test question was "Have you ever been guilty of moral turpitude?" It seemed like the registration process was guilty of moral turpitude.

Registration procedures were the picture of racial discrimination and intimidation. The registrars had the sole power to determine whether a person had correctly filled out the exam. The applicant might be asked to read aloud and interpret a section of the U.S. Constitution to the satisfaction of the registrars, who were sometimes illiterate themselves. That was a sure question to trip up the applicants, even if they passed everything else. How would the registrars determine whether the questions were accurately answered? It was totally subjective. It was simply at the registrars' discretion whether someone passed or failed, and they could decide on a whim, "You didn't pass the test because you didn't interpret the passage right." When the registrants received their results in the mail about a month later, they had no idea which questions were missed. Oddly enough, some schoolteachers, college professors, and professionals failed the test, yet some uneducated laborers passed. It didn't seem to matter to the registrars who got registered; they just had to be able to say that some passed the test and were allowed to register, perhaps one or two each time the office was open, just to stay in compliance with a federal court order and to keep reporters at bay. The registrants had no recourse when they failed except to keep coming back and trying again. I heard that names of registrants were often passed along to the Ku Klux Klan, who continued harassment in their own ways.

Our goal was to get as many people as possible to go to the courthouse and attempt to register in order to demonstrate that the process was discriminatory and to help build a case to eliminate the ludicrous literacy test. When I arrived in Selma, Mrs. Foster was already teaching members of the black community about the literacy test. During the day she worked as a dental hygienist with her brother, Dr. Sullivan Jackson, a dentist with an all-black clientele. He was also a true friend of the movement, often housing leaders including Dr. King, who stayed at his home frequently. His wife was known for her peach cobbler, which was Dr. King's favorite dessert.

At night and on weekends Mrs. Foster devoted her time to helping people practice filling out the registration forms and studying for the literacy tests that they had to pass. She had been trained in citizenship classes sponsored by SCLC in Beaufort, South Carolina. Mrs. Foster had a personal conviction, after being turned down numerous times over an eight-year period before she successfully registered to vote. She was probably responsible for more people passing the literacy test than any other person, and she worked tirelessly training others how to register. Her voter registration classes were held on a regular basis in the Elks Club or in homes. Even though most blacks were systematically denied their voter registration, she gave them the confidence and emotional fortitude they needed to just walk into the office and take the test. Mrs. Foster knew that although her pupils were prepared, they could still be turned down. She gave them the opportunity to learn how to answer the questions, but she educated them also on the process and knowledge of how the system could punish them. The skill and the will were her gifts to each and every individual. She instilled in them the persistence to try again, even when they were turned down, and most important, to understand that they had not failed the test—the system had failed them.

We trained hundreds of applicants, tutoring and instructing them how to read and answer the questions. Even if the card came in the mail that said they didn't pass, they knew that they could answer some of the questions. They had to have a registered person vouch for them to register. When one person vouched for twenty-five people, though, it aroused suspicion and could get the person in trouble. There was just a small handful of black registered voters in Dallas County when I first came to Selma. I'm proud to say that more than nine thousand were registered when I left.

Mass meetings were weekly events that gave large numbers of people a sense of hope and direction. They served a valuable purpose, as masses of supporters gathered together and harmonized our spirits in a common place for a common cause. The meetings accomplished several goals. First, they were educational. Attendees could learn about the issues and the problems that directly affected our lives. It helped us to identify some specific roles of how we could be supportive and partici-pate. Second, they were motivational and inspirational. Powerful speakers presented information and encouraged us through sharing their personal experiences and testimonies. This helped to sustain our commitment and remind us that we were not alone. Third, the meetings gave everyone an opportunity to demonstrate courage. Being present there was an indica-tion that we were not afraid to identify with the cause. It showed others in the community that we were willing to stand up for what was right. The meetings illustrated to adversaries the strength that a group of individu-als had. There was unity of power and a feeling of oneness that the mass meetings created. The gatherings built confidence and assured us that personal sacrifices were not in vain, that in spite of moments of doubt, our goals could be achieved. The meetings kept perceptions positive and allowed us to see potential triumph in times of uncertainty.

Music, the language of the soul, played a major role in developing a sense of togetherness at the mass meetings. It was an opportunity to show the importance of the arts in dramatizing emotions. People transformed their songs of meditation to songs of justice. Singers made up new verses to traditional songs with lyrics that articulated our newfound goals and aspirations. Songs have a way of soothing frustrations, pain, and suffer-ing, but they also can illustrate the power of resistance and determina-tion. Songs such as "We Shall Overcome" said that our will can prevail over negative feelings, and in spite of what happens, we can get through anything. "Ain't Gonna Let Nobody Turn Me Around" proclaimed that we would not be stopped, not even by people who were close to us and afraid for us, as we moved forward in spite of barriers. We drew from the spirituals, which were appropriate since the mass meetings were held in churches, our spiritual home. Sometimes the mass meetings were hard to distinguish from revivals, and although the message was one of political and social issues, the meetings were still connected to our spiritual roots. The mass meeting music was designed to promote involvement rather than to provide a concert or to entertain. We used "call and respond," where the song leader called out the next verse so everyone was involved in the singing. Music was measured not by the quality of the voices but rather by the power of the spirit. The experience was real and the feeling was surreal, deepened by the creative potential of the unconscious mind.

The church was a place that could provide a large enough space for people to come together. Churches weren't financially dependent on outside sources, since they owned the buildings. This is one reason why so many churches were bombed during the course of the civil rights movement. Thankfully, no churches were ever attacked in Selma. However, some churches were threatened with foreclosure on their loans.

Although there were growing numbers at the meetings, all the people who supported the movement were not represented there. The problem with attending the mass meetings was fear of reprisal if identified. Police officers frequently came in and took pictures of the men and women at the meetings and could later recognize them from the photographs. The evidence of their participation could destroy good relationships with whites and could affect them economically. Some were afraid that they or their family members would be punished. Their homes could be bombed, a brother might be beaten, or a mother might be fired from a job. Even if they had personal courage, they were fearful for their loved ones. We learned about some of these incidents only after the campaign. Reprisal had occurred in Birmingham and Mississippi, and everyone was well aware of the suffering that could happen.

Some deacons and trustees who were in leadership positions at the churches did not support the meetings in the beginning. Often they were confronted by whites in authority, who said to them, "What are you people doing over there at those meetings?" "Don't you belong to that church?" "Can't you do something about it?" "Didn't I give your son a job?" "Didn't I take good care of your mother when she worked for me?" These were warnings. The deacons and trustees were reminded of all the things those whites had done for them and that they were putting the whole community in jeopardy by attending the mass meetings.

Part of our strategy to increase the numbers of people at the mass meetings was for each person to bring someone, which would double the attendance. In spite of the flyers we distributed, some people still didn't get the word, so those who were planning to come were directed to scout around and bring more people. Many individuals who never came to mass meetings, such as those in wheelchairs, found creative ways to play a role. I had learned similar strategies from the Nashville sit-ins. For example, there were people who would help in recruiting through phone calls.

Some organized phone trees, a system where each person called the next individual on a list. Volunteers were so clever, they'd call in to talk shows and give comments, and end with, "By the way, there's a mass meeting tonight at six" and give the location. With that one parenthetical statement, they had reached an entire radio audience. One goal was to give as many as possible the opportunity to make their contributions. That is one sign of a movement—massive involvement.

When I first came to Selma and attempted to organize a group to engage in direct action, I encountered resistance and a lack of cooperation. This reluctance to change may have been due to the group's unwillingness to adopt unfamiliar roles and take actions that they were uncertain about or that seemed too risky. I thought that their lack of confidence inadvertently helped to maintain a negative situation in Selma. Their hesitancy to consider another approach may have created an atmosphere of helplessness and left them feeling as though they were stuck in a set of undesirable circumstances beyond their control. No matter how hard I tried to motivate or move the group out of their situation, they unknowingly held on to the status quo. If the situation were to continue, their resistance to change could become their greatest obstacle to change in Selma.

In our efforts to find a location for the first mass meeting I called several churches. They all gave me an emphatic no. There was solid resistance, which meant that the leadership wasn't yet ready for mass movement. This was one issue where a large number of blacks and whites were in full agreement. "Don't bring that mess here," both sides said. They just wanted a quiet and peaceful community where nothing changed and their children were not beaten up and put in jail. The pastors didn't want to cause any problems at their churches because parishioners were fearful that they would be under attack by the white power structure. The peace the people of Selma wanted was a peace where injustice was not disturbed, just tolerated. It was a "don't rock the boat" attitude.

At last I found someone willing and able to host our first mass meeting. Rev. Lewis Lloyd Anderson offered his Tabernacle Baptist Church, but his congregation wouldn't support it. They didn't want their community disturbed, fearing a Birmingham-type response where churches were bombed and children were killed.

Then, something almost miraculous happened when Mr. Boynton died. Even in death, Mr. Boynton found a way to support the voting rights campaign. Mrs. Boynton wanted to have his memorial service at the Tabernacle Baptist Church, where he had been a member for many years. It was the logical place. I approached Mrs. Boynton about the opportunity to combine the memorial service with the mass meeting that we had been trying for weeks to arrange, to no avail. She readily agreed that it would honor her husband because the Dallas County Voters League was his life's work, and he was still the president when he died. He *was* Mr. Voter Registration.

The timing was remarkable. When I explained the plan to have a combined memorial and mass meeting to Rev. Anderson, he wholeheartedly agreed. However, the deacons and trustees of his church were apprehensive about having the service/meeting there. Rev. Anderson boldly stood up to them, saying, "If you don't let us have it in the church, we will meet under that tree outside the church. I will stand up before everyone and announce why we didn't have the meeting in the church, that our deacons and trustees are too afraid." He was fearless. I understood their fear of having the meeting there, but there was no other place to have it. The board finally agreed. This was the beginning—our first mass meeting was finally going to happen.

A few years earlier, Rev. Anderson had been in a life-changing automobile accident. His car was hit by another vehicle, he was knocked unconscious, and his car struck and killed a pedestrian. Because of his outspokenness and involvement in the movement, he was charged with manslaughter, and his case went all the way to the U.S. Supreme Court in March 1960. The Court remanded the case since there was not enough evidence to convict him. They didn't throw it out; they just sent it back to the lower courts. At any point he could have been charged again with the same crime. It cost a lot of money to go through the courts. Having the mass meetings at his church made him stand out and almost invited the authorities to bring charges against him again. For him, it became high risk to be identified with the movement, yet he continued in his commitment. I was reluctant to get him too deeply involved because I was afraid that his life might be ruined.

Rev. Anderson's father-in-law, Dr. William Dinkins, was an influential board member and the first black man to receive a Ph.D. in economics from Brown University in Rhode Island. He came to me and said, "My grandfather laid the bricks for this church, and I don't want to stand by and watch this church be bombed or destroyed."

I was young and outspoken, and I retorted, "I think you should be more concerned about the quality of life of your grandchildren rather than the bricks your grandfather laid." I wouldn't make that kind of remark now; I would have shown more respect for this elderly gentleman. But I said what I felt. Dr. Dinkins and I later became good friends.

Sometimes it's only in the face of death that people find the courage to live out their true convictions. The best way to honor a person's life is to rally around what that person stood for, lived for, and was willing to die for. The flyer for the service/meeting had "Memorial Service for Mr. Boynton" on the top line in large, bold letters. Underneath, "Voter's Registration Meeting" appeared in smaller letters.

I took the mock-up of the flyer over to a black printer and left it to be printed. I called him later and he said, "I can't print this." He didn't want to be associated with this mass rally. I told Rev. Anderson, who paid him a visit and said, "I thought you were a printer. It's not your job to decide what to print, your job is to print what customers give you." But he was so scared that he refused to print it. We took it over to Mr. Edwin Moss, who printed about five hundred flyers, and high school students distributed them all over town. Ed Moss was active in the community—head of the Elks Club, a leader in the Masonic Lodge—and he encouraged me to join the Masons when I first arrived. His family owned the Moss Motel, the only place in town where blacks could stay. He worked in the Catholic Church Office of Development to raise money for the school and hospital. Mr. Moss was instrumental in getting many black business leaders to support the movement financially. He was among the few I could always count on to stand up with me in Selma.

We tried to make people feel comfortable to come to the memorial service. I'm sure some didn't come because it said "Voter Registration" on the flyer and they didn't want to be identified with it. On the other hand, it struck a chord with many. They said, "Mr. Boynton's not here anymore. Maybe I could do something. How would I want to be remembered?" I'm certain some people felt torn and made the decision to attend only at the very last minute. It caused some soul-searching for many people. It struck home if you were not registered to vote. It affected people directly. It was a complex situation, combining these two important events, and we were uncertain where things would go. Could this be the death of our voter registration campaign? The man who symbolized voter registration was no longer here. Would his issue die with him?

What we did was purposeful. Having a voter registration rally was well within the context of Mr. Boynton's goals and desires. It also showed that what he lived for could breathe new life into the campaign. This was the kickoff for the voter registration movement in Selma. We used this occasion to inspire others, a commemoration of Mr. Boynton's life and a celebration of his life's passion played out in the mass meeting. Many had admired him from a distance. Although some didn't believe that he'd be successful in his quest for voter registration, they admired his courage and felt that what he was doing was right. But they didn't want to personally suffer, and they still feared getting involved.

The day of the service/meeting was exceptionally quiet throughout Selma. You could feel the anxiety in the air, yet there was also a tingling anticipation and excitement hanging over the town. As the hour approached, people started trickling into the church. There were no large groups. It looked like people were casually walking down the street, and then they would abruptly take a sharp turn and come in. Police cars were parked outside the church, causing some to come through the back entrance in the basement to avoid being seen. It was a real test of wills. Should they be afraid to go to church to attend their friend's memorial service? Some had to struggle with that. Many dressed in street clothes rather than their Sunday best, as they ordinarily would to attend a funeral.

As it came closer to the time the meeting was scheduled to start, curiosity heightened and the intense atmosphere reached a crescendo. It was the first test to see whether people were ready to break the barrier of fear. If their employers asked, they had a convenient rationale for being there, since it was a memorial service. At the same time, those who only wanted to attend the memorial service had to attend the rally. It was impossible to participate in one without the other. The combination gave people the freedom to gather. We were celebrating Mr. Boynton's life, not his death, and everyone knew that he lived for the cause of voter registration. So how could we ignore what his life stood for?

About 350 people attended, but many just couldn't get there. I heard that the police had blocked off several streets surrounding the church and even knocked out taillights so cars could be pulled over afterward for safety violations. Sheriff Clark was snapping photographs of everyone entering the church so that he could later identify who was there—another scare tactic. In spite of those deterrents, people still poured into the church, and young people even crawled under the houses that were on blocks in order to evade the sheriff's notice.

There was one powerful incident that day that I distinctly remember. As the service was just about ready to begin, I was still standing outside on the front steps of the church. A sided flatbed truck drove to the front of the church. It was loaded with about twenty young white men armed with wooden table legs, ready for action. They jumped off the back of the truck and headed toward the church to disrupt the service. The group of boys had started up the steps toward me, and I knew I was about to be clobbered or killed. When I saw the hate in their eyes and their determined strides, I felt like I had experienced this before. I had the same feelings when the mob came after a group of us during the Nashville sit-ins. And even worse, another incident flashed before my eyes—being beaten by a few attackers in an angry crowd at the Montgomery bus station during the Freedom Rides. How well I remember my throat closing and the difficulty I had swallowing when I saw those determined boys moving my way. Although my breath was shallow, I purposely took a deep breath to prepare myself for an attack. I knew I had to be ready for whatever was to come. I had to transfer my fear to resistance, as I had been trained to do.

Suddenly a car screeched to a halt in the middle of the street. The door flew open and an older white man dressed in civilian clothes jumped out and shouted orders: "You boys get back on that truck and get out of here! Now!" To my amazement, the young men stopped in mid-stride, turned around, and sheepishly walked back to the truck, heads down. The man stayed there until every single guy climbed back into the truck and drove away.

The power of this man's presence at that moment single-handedly saved the situation from escalating into mob violence, saved the mass meeting, and possibly changed the course of history. I later found out that the man was a former football coach at the all-white Parrish High School in Selma. A few of those young men had been his players and now worked at the table factory. If the first mass meeting had resulted in violence, it's unlikely that the voting rights campaign in Selma could have continued. Somehow, we found support in the most unlikely places. There were a number of whites in Selma who didn't agree with the violence that was used against blacks who were attempting to exercise their rights. They expressed their personal concerns in various ways. This coach was an example of one courageous white supporter. The experience gave me yet another sense of hope.

Fortunately, most people were already in the church and didn't know what was happening outside until afterward. This mass meeting began with a choir singing, then a time of devotion and prayer, similar to a Sunday service. Rev. Anderson welcomed everyone and stated, "This occasion is to memorialize Mr. Boynton and to honor his service and contributions to the community." There were prayers for the Boynton family. We sang freedom songs. We sang church spirituals. We sang songs with familiar tunes with the lyrics changed to words of freedom and justice. Seamlessly, Rev. Anderson transitioned from remembering Mr. Boynton to giving information about where to go for classes to prepare for the literacy tests. I believe that every person there had lifted spirits and a renewed sense of commitment, determination, and courage. Mainly, we helped them to realize that they did not stand alone in the efforts of their convictions. It was the best blend of tribute and rally, and I'm certain that Mr. Boynton would have been proud to know what was taking place. It felt like he was smiling down on us from heaven.

We invited James Forman to be the main guest speaker. He was chosen because he was the executive secretary of SNCC and was a fiery and passionate speaker. Although he was senior to me in age and experience, I had recruited him for the position of executive secretary and greatly admired and respected him. Because of Jim, SNCC came alive and thrived. A former professor at Roosevelt University in Chicago, Jim was bright and energetic. He could have pursued an academic career, but he chose instead to cast his lot with the civil rights movement. He could be classified as a militant, and he later wrote an autobiography titled *The*

Making of Black Revolutionaries. This included some of my Selma report, which gave a glimpse into a day in the life of a SNCC worker—and that worker was me. Jim described himself as believing in nonviolence as a tactic but not necessarily a way of life, and he often disagreed with Dr. King on various other issues. He had strong opinions and was given to debate and argument, yet he was always conciliatory. His political views fell about midway between Dr. King's and those of the more radical Malcolm X. He had a deep appreciation of the history of the struggle, and extensive knowledge. Although he was older than most of the SNCC students, he was always respectful of the fact that we were the ones who would carry the movement forward. He gave advice, counsel, and guidance, but not direct orders. I was proud to show him what had been accomplished in Selma in a short period of time, especially since the SNCC organizers didn't expect any change to occur. It was also a way to give visibility to the campaign in Selma. I named my first son, Jim, after him, because I didn't know what fate might befall me in the midst of this Selma experience, and I wanted my son to have a godfather who was committed to the movement. And there was no one who was more dedicated than James Forman.

That night Jim stepped up to the pulpit and was an imposing presence, tall and stocky with a broad face and eyes that seemed to peer deeply into each of our souls. He focused right in on the main issue of the community, which was systematic discrimination of black voters in Selma. He encouraged lots of interaction with those there.

He asked, "How many of you have tried to register to vote?" Several hands went up. "How many were successful in registering?" Only a few hands remained raised. "How many will commit to going down to the courthouse and attempting to register?" Many hands waved high in the air.

Jim spoke about overcoming fear and complacency that paralyzed people and prohibited them from taking a stand that they knew was right. He talked about the history of oppression, which, he said, "will continue until each one of us decides to do something about it." He addressed the issue of our constitutional rights and how we shouldn't allow anyone to take them away. He said, "This is our country and many have fought and died for the rights that we are being denied. Let us make sure their deaths were not in vain. We must be prepared to make a sacrifice. Freedom is not given to us on a silver platter; even the limited freedom we enjoy now is because of people in the past who have suffered, bled, and died." Jim said that the government's responsibility is to protect our rights. "But," he said, "we can't wait for the government and should attempt to exercise our rights now. We cannot wait. If we wait, our children will never enjoy the benefits of their birthrights. We must make democracy real, not just words on fine parchment paper. The Constitution gives us our rights, but unless we attempt to exercise them, we lose those rights. They will be taken away from us." There were lots of amens of support. He urged people to go and register to vote in large numbers, to take their relatives and friends. Forman shocked the audience by saying, "Blood may have to flow down the streets of Selma before we get the right to vote." One pastor tried to soften the tone afterward by saying we should not put all the blame on white people. We should take more responsibility in disciplining our children. His remarks got no response from the audience.

The people of Selma had never heard anything like that speech. It was soul stirring, conscience crashing, and life changing. It accomplished all I desired. Afterward, people commented, "This is a new day." Some proclaimed, "Things will never be the same in Selma. A change is going to come."

A week or so after the first mass meeting, I was driving home from a voter registration meeting. Flashing lights in my rearview mirror caught my attention and brought a lump to my throat. There had been some backlash after the first mass meeting, with blacks given tickets for broken taillights. Because Sheriff Clark had taken pictures of people entering the church, he knew who to target. I was pulled over by the police and asked to show my driver's license. The officers looked surprised when I showed them a legitimate Alabama driver's license, as they assumed that I wouldn't have changed it yet. They knew I was new in town from another state. They had a lengthy discussion between themselves, then they told me I was under arrest but wouldn't tell me why. A policeman drove my car, making it seem like it was planned ahead of time. I didn't want anyone driving my 1948 Chevrolet because it was a unique car for that period. It had a fluid drive and a clutch on the steering column, not on the floor. It was finicky, and if you didn't know how to drive it properly, you could strip the gears. I heard the officer grinding the gears, and I was distraught. Another legitimate concern was that they might plant something in my car and charge me with the crime.

I suspect that when their plan didn't work to charge me with driving without an Alabama license, they decided to charge me with something else—vagrancy. When I moved from Tennessee to Alabama, I changed my license immediately because I knew what had happened to Dr. King earlier. The reason he didn't go on the Freedom Rides was that he was out of jail on probation after being arrested and charged for improper registration of his car, since he hadn't changed his license when he moved to Atlanta from Montgomery. I wanted to make sure this didn't happen to me. When I had taken the driver's license test about a month earlier, the examiner graded it and yelled out to all the staff people in the back, "This n***** done made a hundred on this here test." Everybody came out of their offices and looked at me in surprise, as if it were impossible for a black person to make a perfect score. In those days the driver's license was a postcard (see fig. 13 in the photo gallery). You had to take a pair of scissors and cut out your license after receiving it in the mail.

The vagrancy charge was curious to me. It didn't make sense to be charged for vagrancy while driving a car. Mrs. Boynton bailed me out of jail. A federal court reporter was assigned to follow this trial because of my involvement with the Voter Registration Campaign. The U.S. Department of Justice was making sure that the action against me could be cited as an instance of the state interfering with someone who was helping people register to vote.

When I was arrested for vagrancy, Attorneys J. L. Chestnut and Solomon Seay immediately came to my defense. There were only a few black lawyers in the South during this period who handled cases for the NAACP, and they were generally labeled "civil rights" attorneys. Mr. Seay and Mr. Chestnut were two of them. Attorney Seay practiced in Montgomery, and Attorney Chestnut practiced in Selma. They often partnered with each other on cases, as their combined forces yielded more power.

Solomon Seay was born in Montgomery from a long line of educated social activists. His father was a renowned preacher and adviser to Dr. King during the Montgomery Bus Boycott, and his mother was a schoolteacher. His uncle was an attorney who had received a law degree from

Columbia University. He earned a law degree from Howard University, receiving a strong foundation in constitutional law. He often said that he wanted to make the world a little better than it was when he grew up, and I can certainly attest that he did.

Mr. Chestnut was considered by most to be a smart lawyer, though some disagreed with this public reputation. Some thought instead that he was cocky, but I thought he earned his right to be cocky. He had a slight build, not too tall, but he had a deep baritone voice. When he spoke it had a thunderous quality, and you could feel the vibration and hear the echo. He was unreserved in his intolerance for rhetoric and always spoke straight to the point. His manner was more like a judge than a lawyer: he sounded like he was pronouncing judgment on the court. Always well dressed in court, he wore a classy suit and looked as professional as any New York lawyer. When he received his law degree from Howard University, he was already committed to the civil rights struggle, and he became Selma's first black lawyer. Although he could have joined a high-powered law firm anywhere in the country, he made a conscious choice to practice in Selma, where he was born, believing that he could serve the cause best right there. He told me that he anticipated future legal battles taking place in Dallas County, and his intuition was right. I have deep admiration for him and hold him in the highest esteem. I will always be grateful that this courageous and noble man used his knowledge of the law to help hundreds of activists get out of jail and represented them through their trials, including me on several occasions. He was always supportive of my efforts.

These two lawyers were already well-known civil rights attorneys and commanded respect from all quarters. At my trial, there was a complete role reversal for Sheriff Jim Clark as they interrogated him in cross-examination. Even though he was the one who ordered my arrest, I actually felt embarrassed for him with the questions they asked. "What was the reason Rev. LaFayette was stopped?" "How could an officer come to a conclusion that Rev. LaFayette had no visible means of support while driving his car?" "Did you check his refrigerator to see if there was any food to warrant a vagrancy charge?" "Did you check his employment records to see if he had a regular job and an income?"

Sheriff Clark said that he had received phone calls complaining that

Rev. LaFayette had been begging for food. Mr. Chestnut said, "I'm sure you have a very efficient office staff who keeps good records. Do you have a log of these phone calls?"

The sheriff replied, "No. I don't keep any logs."

Mr. Chestnut looked shocked. "You mean to tell me that you send your men out to arrest folks whenever someone calls in complaints?"

Clark explained, "Well, they said that Rev. LaFayette asked for food at the meeting." Everyone at the mass meetings knew me very well. I sometimes joked with them about who was inviting me to dinner that week. The truth of the matter was that Jim Clark had surveillance at the mass meetings and took my comments out of context in order to find a reason to arrest me. When he realized that he couldn't charge me on the license issue, he had to think hard about what he could charge me with. Vagrancy was all he could come up with, and he ended up looking foolish. It was so ridiculous and obvious that this was a trumped-up charge that Judge James A. Hare quickly threw the case out of court.

"Case dismissed," the judge announced, and he pounded his gavel hard. This was the first case of all of my arrests where I was found not guilty in the first court of law. Usually in civil rights cases, when you are arrested, you are found guilty and have to win on appeal. In fact the defense lawyers would go into court with documentation as if they were planning to go to the Supreme Court, citing Supreme Court cases, laying the foundation for the impending appeal.

I had begun to experience the same type of treatment that the local residents had come to know and expect. Initially an outsider, I was part of their suffering now, one of them. I no longer had to ask for their stories; I now was beginning to collect my own. I wondered what would happen next. I felt very good about having the case dismissed, and I was proud of those two young lawyers.

Mr. Chestnut's authority was widespread throughout the Selma community. One time many years later, several of us civil rights activists were in Selma and had a discrepancy at a motel. They were overcharging us. I commented, "Perhaps we need to call Attorney Chestnut to resolve this problem." The proprietor immediately said, "That won't be necessary. We'll work this out."

In the beginning I was organizing the mass meetings, but it was difficult finding churches that would host them. Mr. Moss told me that some conservative black ministers wanted to be the leaders of the movement since they were leaders in the community. However, they hadn't yet taken the leadership for the voting rights cause and they were scared. I was more than happy for them to assume some leadership roles and become involved in organizing the mass meetings. This would have helped me. Yet I was also apprehensive about their leadership. Would they try to hold the people back in their state of apathy and fear? Another problem was in the risks they would have to take to host the meetings in their churches and the repercussions that might follow.

I formulated a creative strategy for refocusing this group in Selma—a strategy I now call "deliberate leadership role reversal." They were initially reluctant to follow my lead, or to engage in a course of action that would secure them their constitutional right to vote. But by organizing them against me as their leader, I was able to transform this group of conservative ministers to exert their own leadership, to cooperate with me, and to take action. This resulted in a strengthening of the group and their willingness to step forward toward the goal. As Dr. King frequently said, "Sometimes it is best to lead from the rear." With the help of Mr. Moss, this was the strategy I used with the group of conservative black ministers.

Mr. Moss, a liaison in the Catholic Church, met with this group of black pastors on the issue of who should be the leaders to help in the voting rights campaign. When the ministers made statements such as "We are the ones who should be the leaders. Rev. LaFayette is an outsider, so he shouldn't be coming in here and leading us," Mr. Moss agreed that they should take the leadership. They decided to have secret weekly meetings in their homes, beginning with a few ministers and gradually adding more. As they added new ministers week after week, the pool of conservative ministers would be gradually diminished and more moderate ministers would be included. Each week Mr. Moss called me and gave a progress report. At the meetings, Mr. Moss encouraged the ministers to take a stand on voter registration, although they weren't sure about it. One thing was certain—they wanted to be the leaders.

Rev. Anderson came to me, worried, and said, "Rev. LaFayette, did you know that some clergy are meeting and they are against you? They feel you were taking over their role as leaders in the community."

I said, "Yes, I'm aware of that."

He asked, "What should we do about it?"

I said, "Don't worry about it. Eventually, you'll be invited to one of the meetings. Just wait and see." I explained the process, that at each meeting they invited more ministers.

He said, "No, goodness, no, it's the wrong crowd. I can tell you right now, those preachers would never invite me, because I'm not conservative enough."

In the meantime, I found out where they were going to meet on one particular night. We were desperate for a mass meeting but had no location for it. We hadn't met in almost three weeks and I knew how important it was to keep momentum. Mass meetings were one way to keep people encouraged and inspired and communicating with each other. So I got the phone number of where they were meeting. The night of the meeting I called the house. The person who answered the phone was another minister who was attending the meeting and happened to be sitting near the phone. In an innocent voice I said, "This is Rev. LaFayette. I want to know if we can have a mass meeting next Thursday at your church." He hesitated and then said, "Yes, you can have a mass meeting then at my church."

I thanked him for stepping up and showing bold leadership and courage. He said, "Hold on a minute." I heard muffled voices in the background, and after a while he came back on the receiver and said, "The following week you can have it at Rev. ———'s church." I lined up a whole month of mass meetings scheduled at various churches with one phone call, and I had been trying for weeks to arrange just one meeting. It just so happened that the person who answered the phone was a moderate and took the initiative to line up multiple meetings on the spot. They had been boosting themselves up by being the leaders. Sure enough, they all came through, and it opened up Selma. I never had to worry about finding churches for mass meetings again.

As I anticipated, the group eventually invited Rev. Anderson to join. He was shocked. I smiled and said, "I told you so." He never expected it and was glad to be included. When he had had his accident a few years earlier, he had received no support from the other ministers and had had to stand alone. He began to attend the meetings and helped drive the group toward the goal of voter registration. Now he had some support.

A mass meeting was organized at Brown Chapel, and the day of the meeting the minister called and said, "We can't have the meeting here tonight. We just can't have it." The minister of Brown Chapel wanted to have the meeting, but he received a call from the bishop and was ordered to cancel it. We scrambled around quickly to find a new location. Attorney Chestnut attended the First Baptist Church, which was less than a block down the street, and he helped arrange the meeting there. As people arrived at Brown Chapel, we directed them to the neighboring church. We had many more mass meetings at the First Baptist Church. Churches often received pressure from outside forces, and ministers took great risks to host the mass meetings. Some of the trustees and board members were pressured by the white business community and endured suffering and intimidation as they stood up for their beliefs.

The main speaker at the second mass meeting was Mrs. Lois Reeves, a woman from outside Selma. It was important at first to have speakers who were not from the Selma community, so they couldn't be ostracized. Mrs. Reeves was the wife of the pastor of the Westminster Presbyterian Church in Tuskegee, Alabama. I got to know her when she hosted me while I was doing research in Tuskegee. We stayed up at night talking about social issues, particularly topics related to the oppression of black people. She was very well spoken and impressed me as someone who was not afraid to take a stand. I hadn't really thought about her as being a mass meeting speaker, but I needed to bring in someone who was close by and willing. When I called and asked her she said, "Of course, I'd be happy to come. I'm ready to do whatever I can."

The church was overflowing, and even the churchyard was packed. Mrs. Reeves was an inspiring speaker but also outspoken, so I didn't know what the repercussions might be when the white community heard about the meeting. She had driven up to Selma alone. I wanted someone to go back with her to Tuskegee, but she insisted that she would be fine. When she got into her car that night following the meeting, I feared for her safety on the two-hour drive home. She called me when she arrived safely. What a relief! I took a deep breath, dropped to my knees, and said, "Thank you, Lord."

We organized a mass meeting at the Mount Zion AME Church. The ministers, even though they wanted to be leaders, weren't ready to take a strong stand by making a speech. As organizers, we didn't want to put people on the spot or push people because that would make them defensive. We encouraged them to take small steps, which at this point meant simply hosting the mass meetings. Then a number of other churches began to open their doors.

We continued to have outside speakers at our meetings. Miss Ella Baker didn't hesitate to come when we invited her, and she spoke forcefully and eloquently, her deep voice commanding. I was proud to see women leaders step forward at a time when it was important to show courage. Our modern-day Harriet Tubman, Miss Baker, too, devoted her life to helping people gain their freedom. Some churches didn't allow women to speak from the pulpit, but because the gathering was designated as a mass meeting, the administrators at the church allowed it. Miss Baker showed that people could stand tall in a moment of crisis regardless of one's height, gender, or color. The shouts of "We want freedom!" rang with multiple echoes.

We invited Rev. James Bevel as the main speaker for one of the mass meetings. He was a respected colleague of Dr. King's and known for being a gifted planner and organizer who was currently working in the Mississippi Voting Rights Movement for SCLC. Although he had some debatable postures, he had a number of strengths that Dr. King appreciated and needed. Dr. King recognized Bevel's strategic thinking and effective speaking, as he was practical and convincing. When he took a position, he was adamant about it and presented a concrete moral and ethical basis to support his position. He was radical and extremist in his thinking; often his thoughts and decisions were considered unorthodox and controversial, and many of his ideas and conclusions required modification or some elimination. But Dr. King realized when making decisions it is always good to have a point and a counterpoint. Because Bevel had the mind of a lawyer and could debate both sides of any issue effectively, Dr. King quietly listened to Bevel's assessment of situations and often took away portions of his ideas and adapted them, referring to him as a genius for his intellect. Some of Bevel's ideas had a strong impact on the movement.

During the Birmingham movement, also known as "Project C" for "confrontation," there was a debate as to whether children should be allowed to participate in the marches and demonstrations. The safety commissioner in Birmingham, Bull Connor, was prepared to release police dogs and use fire hoses on the protesters as well as beat them with billy clubs. Bevel's argument was that children should be allowed to participate because they were the ones who would benefit from the change. They would also feel empowered if they helped to make the change. The other side of the argument was that we as adults should take the responsibility to protect our children rather than allow them to be brutalized. The children wholeheartedly sided with Bevel. However, many people would have been horrified if they had known the extent to which Bevel wanted to use the children: as he said, "not just the older teenagers but also the junior high students on down to 'the babies' just out of kindergarten." Of course this didn't happen. But more than one thousand students did protest and were jailed, by their own choice. There was huge confrontation in this movement, with the jails overflowing and the television cameras running to show the entire world. The business community in this town was afraid of the damage the publicity was doing as well as the physical damage that might happen to the stores and shops, and business owners agreed to hire more blacks as well as desegregate the lunch counters. This agreement was made against the wishes of the sheriff's department and the city government.[2]

I noticed that Dr. King and Jim Bevel were similar in a few ways: First, they were bright, deductive thinkers, looking first at the whole picture then at the smaller components, appreciating that the individual ingredients made up the larger picture. Second, they looked at associations and made connections that might not immediately meet the eye. Third, they fully understood the importance of nonviolent confrontation. Having theological backgrounds, they could relate the scriptures to the ordinary people we were attempting to reach in the rural South. Speaking the southern vernacular, Dr. King and Bevel could interpret the scriptures to them in a way that rationalized and supported direct action in contrast to the way some of the Selma preachers had previously interpreted the scriptures to keep people inactive. For example, they could compare the situation of the oppressed Israelites to the blacks in the South. In this context, they could help people gain a comfortable stance for going to jail. Civil disobedience could be phrased in a modern context rather than being seen as an antiquated idea. Last, and most important, Dr. King and Jim Bevel had undaunted courage.

It turned out to be an interesting mass meeting when Bevel spoke. Earlier that week Bob's Tavern had experienced an incident where the beer distributors had come by to pick up the empties. "I can't sell you any more beer, Bob," the distributor told him. The beer distributors had decided to boycott Bob because they had been informed that he was attending mass meetings. It hurt Bob financially not to be allowed to sell beer in the middle of a long, hot summer. So before Bevel spoke, we told him about this problem. At the meeting, Bevel addressed the issue: "I understand the beer distributor is boycotting Bob and won't bring him any more beer to sell. I'm going to tell y'all the truth. I like beer and I often drink it. But I'm going to stop drinking beer if they are going to stop selling beer to Bob's Tavern because he attended a mass meeting. How many folks here will join me?" A large part of the church, including the deacons and elderly women, stood up and agreed to stop drinking beer. Bevel had that kind of influence on people. He was a born leader. The next morning, the beer distributor came by and told Bob they would sell him beer again. Clearly, he had heard about the potential boycott and couldn't risk having his beer sit on the shelves in other stores or taverns.

By this time people understood that if they became united in their strength, if they stood together, even if they had to suffer and deny themselves, their combined voices had more force and power. Bob was not alone. That was the clear message. When others stood with Bob, the beer company changed its mind and resumed delivery. The community that supported him recognized that solidarity was the only way they could defeat this oppressive action against him. Once they saw the real impact they could have, they began to believe that other things could change. The black people of Selma were coming into a new awareness of the power of unity. Indeed, things had changed. The change started with them. In many instances the voices of the conservative ministers were in conflict with the outside speakers. However, as time went on, the separate voices blended together to become one voice. Although community members went to different churches, they lived in the same neighborhoods and worked on the same jobs; their children went to the same school; and they all attended the same mass meetings. When great numbers of church members became actively involved in the mass meetings, the ministers were pulled along to join in to support their congregation. This was critical for the progress and success of the Voting Rights Movement.

To keep the movement nonviolent and to prepare large groups for protests, teaching was done on a mass basis from the pulpit. I gave admonitions in the mass meetings to follow the discipline of the leaders. The people were told that if they were to protest, they were to be nonviolent and not strike back because it would tarnish the movement. I asked that if they felt they couldn't do this, they would not participate. If they felt they couldn't be nonviolent, then they contributed in other ways. They wanted to see change, and over time they became confident in the leadership.

Fortunately, people had already watched many situations on television of protesters not hitting back, so we referred to those incidents. They had seen examples of violence from the opponents in Birmingham and didn't want this to happen in their home city of Selma. Because the directives were coming from clergymen in the church, from me, and from others, they felt spiritually connected. Most had grown up in the church and knew the precepts of God's love, and they viewed the challenge as an opportunity to put religion into practice, applying the nonviolent responses that they were learning. The mass meeting speakers used biblical references that had been a part of their lives since they were children growing up. The tone was that this was something sacred and that they were called upon now to do the extraordinary. The songs and the words that they felt were sacred stirred their spirits and gave them the fortitude they needed to endure. They were prepared. There was a strong feeling of collective community, where people resolved, "If my neighbors are going to march, I will march with them. I can do this too." People thought they would try it, and when faced with the test, they passed.

At the end of every mass meeting I breathed a sigh of relief. When the last person left and the lights were turned out, I was always grateful that there had been no incidents with law enforcement. I never knew from one meeting to the next what to expect from Sheriff Clark's office. I felt that each mass meeting broke through another layer of fear. As attendance grew I saw that even Sheriff Clark's scare tactics of parking outside the church and photographing people couldn't stop the building momentum. People usually arrived in groups, as there was more safety in numbers; individuals often walked in with families, clubs, organizations, or church groups. Somehow, people found a way.

4

Central Alabama Heats Up

The time is always right to do what is right.
—Dr. Martin Luther King Jr.

Benny Tucker, a student at Selma University, became actively involved in the Selma campaign. I often let him use my car, fondly called the "movement car." He was out running office errands one day and had a wreck. He ran smack into the back of a car at a traffic light, unquestionably his fault. The other driver turned out to be a white schoolteacher who lived in the county. Her husband was a farmer. The very fact that my car had rear-ended this woman could be fuel for a fire that no amount of water could extinguish. I was on pins and needles waiting for the police to come and arrest me. I was afraid that the woman might have had whiplash and that they could take everything I had and run me out of town. After a few days I got a phone call from a deputy sheriff about the accident. I braced myself for the worst, praying the woman was not hurt.

The deputy told me, "I know the husband of the woman who was driving the car. I talked to him and the man said he doesn't want to cause any trouble. All he wants is for his car to be repaired. The farmer's going to get an estimate of how much it will cost and get back in touch with me." He told me not to discuss this with anyone else, that it was a private conversation between the two of us. He also said that the farmer was an older man with a hearing problem and his wife was a younger woman.

A few days later the deputy called to let me know that the cost of repairs was going to be $150. The next thing he said was, "Tomorrow, meet me and the farmer at 4:30 in the morning outside of town on a rural road to pay the money in cash. Come alone and don't tell anyone about this meeting—no one." I wanted to get this situation resolved. I hadn't been able to eat or sleep for days. This request seemed odd, and I didn't know what was going to happen. Even though the deputy told me not to tell anyone, I told Mrs. Boynton, and she advised me not to go, fearing for my life.

Only a fine line exists between courage and foolishness. I reasoned back and forth. Should I go, should I not? What would happen if I went? What would happen if I didn't go? What was their real plan? I knew I had to pay the money I owed the farmer for the car, that much was certain. Maybe this deputy was honest, but I didn't know. I figured that he was being secretive either because he didn't want Jim Clark to find out that he was helping me or because he was planning to sabotage me. Finally, after much deliberation, I decided to trust the deputy sheriff and to believe in the farmer. I took a high risk and whispered a few prayers throughout a sleepless night. At 4:15 A.M. I climbed into my car and drove out of town to the designated meeting place, alone. The night was a dark, eerie gray with a half moon edging in and out of clouds. In the distance I saw two lone vehicles pulled off the side of the road. I parked behind the farmer's pickup truck and the deputy's car. My mind flooded with concerns. Would they accept the money and then it would all be over? Would they set me up, claiming I had money to buy drugs? Would they plant a gun in my hand, alleging that they had to shoot me in self-defense? I was ready to die, at the worst. But really, the worst would have been being put in prison for a trumped-up charge or beaten up and crippled for life. It was in their hands. I knew how difficult it was to win justice in the courts of Selma. I put my trust in God and prayed a silent prayer.

Taking a few deep breaths, I waited in my car a few minutes, looking around to see who else might show up. My car door moaned as I pushed it open and climbed out into darkness. I pulled the money out of my pocket, fifteen worn ten-dollar bills. Looking him directly in the eye, I handed the cash to the deputy. No words were spoken. In silence the deputy passed the money to the farmer sitting in the shadows of his truck cab. I turned around, expecting them to shoot me in the back of the head, walked steadfastly to my car, got in, and drove away. All the way home my heart pounded, and I anticipated that police cars might swarm me and set me up on false charges. I waited every day to see how this incident was going to unfold. Nothing happened.

The only thing I can surmise is that the deputies who were assigned as surveillance at the mass meetings were leaning slightly toward empathy for our cause. They would sit in the back and convey what was going on by walkie-talkie to Sheriff Jim Clark, who would be outside in his car. Some people hung tin foil from the lights in the ceiling to interfere with the walkie-talkie signals. I told them to take the foil down. I said, "These officers have to do their jobs. Anybody could go tell Jim Clark what was going on, including some black folks who do that anyway. Let the deputy sheriffs do what they are here to do." I always tried to give them a boost in the meetings because one goal is to win the opponents over, not alienate people. I often said, "These deputy sheriffs have to work overtime here at the mass meeting and we know they're not getting paid overtime. When we get the right to vote, we're going to make sure that they get paid for the jobs they do, equal justice for all. They need their money to buy food for their families, shoes for their children." I think the deputies liked what they heard and began to appreciate me as a human being, no longer viewing me as just an agitator. That deputy sheriff might not have been in favor of what we were doing, and I don't think he was. But out of respect, he took a risk to help me, and he could have lost his job over the incident. Winning people over once again paid off, as it often does many times over, and furthered our cause.

I can't know for sure, but I was told that five deputies had resigned from the sheriff's department during my time in Selma. Although I don't know their reasons, I wonder whether they might have resigned because they could no longer carry out Sheriff Clark's orders to attack innocent people who simply wanted basic human rights.

On June 12, 1963, there was a planned attempt to assassinate Benjamin Elton Cox in Louisiana, Medgar Evers in Mississippi, and me in Alabama. We were civil rights leaders in three different states. There were many civil rights leaders throughout the South, so I'm not sure why we were chosen. That night we were all three slated for attack at approximately the same time, with intent to kill. This was later referred to as the tri-state conspiracy.

Ben was working in New Orleans with CORE. That night was not unlike many other nights when his life had been threatened. But he happened to be out of town. That chance trip out of the city saved his life. When I talked to him later about the plot that the FBI had explained to me, he acknowledged how lucky he was to have been away. We've been friends for many years, and sometimes he sends me a "deathday" card instead of a birthday card!

Rev. Benjamin Elton Cox began his life in the civil rights movement at the young age of fifteen, protesting at an A&W drive-in in Illinois. The next year he became an organizer for the NAACP, helping to establish youth chapters as a national field secretary. He had to drop out of high school to support his family, being the sixteenth of seventeen children, yet he was determined to get a high school degree, which he eventually did. He went on to complete college in North Carolina and then was successful in finishing his theological studies to become the pastor of Pilgrim Congregational Church in High Point, North Carolina. He didn't waste any time in getting actively involved in the community there and served on the school desegregation committee.

In 1960, after the famous Greensboro Four's lunch counter sit-in, Ben galvanized other groups of high school students to participate in more demonstrations in the Greensboro area and was quite successful in integrating several establishments, such as McDonald's. No stranger to jail, he was arrested many times, yet it never suppressed his commitment to the civil rights cause. He founded the first High Point chapter of CORE and was sent to Washington, D.C., to be trained in nonviolent direct action. In May 1961 Ben and twelve others began the original Freedom Rides, riding the bus out of Washington, D.C., to New Orleans.

When these conspiracy acts occur, they are not just intended for the ones being attacked; they are meant to send a strong message to others. The arbitrators want to show what will happen if civil rights workers continue their actions. For this reason, most such attacks were aimed at killing individuals, rather than using bombings that would kill hundreds.

The second attack the night of June 12 was on Medgar Evers, a man of enormous courage. I first met him when I was on the Freedom Rides. When Jim Bevel and I remained in Jackson, Mississippi, to recruit Freedom Riders, Medgar helped us to establish an office. He was the executive secretary of the NAACP in Mississippi, headquartered in Jackson on Lynch Street. Lynch was the name of the black legislator elected during the Reconstruction period, but to most black people "lynch" was a constant reminder of the worst kind of brutality that blacks had suffered. Retired from the military, Medgar was efficient and well organized. The NAACP was strong in Mississippi, even throughout the rural areas, where there had been a number of attacks on local chapters. Many homes of the officers had been bombed, and several leaders had been killed.

Medgar's work allowed him to aid many sharecroppers in Jackson. I remember one night I stayed at his office while he left in a pickup truck to clandestinely rescue a family. A white farm owner was sending for the tenant farmer's teenage daughter to spend the night with him. The black farmer was so enraged that he was almost driven to violence. He thought a better decision would be to secretly leave the farm that night with his family. It was difficult for them to leave because at the end of the year there was always a negative balance and tenant farmers had to continue to work to pay off the balance. Medgar was able to get the family off the farm and send them on a northbound bus. This was risky business because had he been caught, Medgar certainly would have been killed. It seemed like the Underground Railroad all over again.

Medgar was a natural leader and a well-rounded individual. In college he did everything from playing football to participating on the debate team to singing in the school choir to running track. His accomplishments were honored by his being listed in *Who's Who among Students in American Universities and Colleges*. He organized a boycott of local gas stations that refused to allow blacks to use the restroom facilities. Later he was instrumental in helping James Meredith succeed in entering and desegregating the University of Mississippi in the fall of 1962 after mentoring him in strategy for a couple of years.

Death threats became a part of Medgar's life, but he never stopped his work. The weeks before he died he was targeted with increased hostility and threats. His home was bombed with a Molotov cocktail thrown into his carport, and he was almost hit by a speeding car when he came out of his office. The day of the planned attacks, President Kennedy gave a rousing speech on television that lent support to the civil rights movement. Medgar returned home from a meeting with NAACP lawyers. As he got out of his car in his carport, carrying an armload of T-shirts that read "Jim Crow Must Go," he was shot in the back, and he died at the hospital within an hour. So many people in the country mourned the death of this great man. He was honored with a military funeral and burial in Arlington National Cemetery.

The third attack on June 12 was slated for me. I had just returned from a mass meeting and pulled into my driveway. I saw a pink and white Chevrolet, which had a fantail like the '57 model, parked across the street from my house. There were two white guys, one at the steering wheel and the other looking under the hood. I didn't pay too much attention to them as I was tired and heading home ready to sleep.

The night was dark; a large tree shaded one streetlight, casting gray shadows. As I was getting papers out of the backseat of my two-door '48 Chevy, I suddenly heard leaves cracking behind me. My immediate thought was, "Oh no, I'm going to be attacked." I spun around to face my opponent, as I had been trained to do. A huge fellow was approaching. He towered over me. My eyes might have been in line with his collarbone. He had a crew cut and wore a tight T-shirt with rolled-up sleeves that showed off his substantial arm muscles. He said, "Buddy, how much would you charge for a push?" I was relieved to hear that he only wanted a push, because I thought he wanted my life. I told him I wouldn't charge anything, that I'd be glad to help him out. We learn in life that it is important to give each person the benefit of the doubt and not to judge a person based on differences. It is also important to be prepared for those persons who would seek to do you bodily harm.

I got back into my car and pulled up behind his, ready to give him a push. The man closed the hood and then had a long conversation with the driver. Impatient, I wondered what the problem was. I was anxious to get this over. Finally, he came over to my car, looked at the bumpers, then hesitated. I asked if the bumpers matched okay and he said, "Maybe you'd better come take a look." It seemed odd, but I got out and bent over to check the bumpers.

Suddenly, a crushing blow to my head sent me flying to the pavement, flat out. I still recall every detail of the next few minutes. I jumped back up quickly and faced him because that is the nonviolent way to respond so your adversary does not succeed in his attack. The second blow was equally devastating as a blunt instrument cracked my head and sent me straight back to the pavement in the middle of the street. He pounded me with the butt of a pistol, metal against bone. By sheer will I staggered up again, trying to look him in the eye. The third time he came down on the top of my head with steel, knocking me down again. My eyes filled with blood and he became blurry in my vision.

Then I saw the gun. When the muzzle's black hole pointed straight at my head, I shouted for my neighbor, "Red," who lived above me. Even in the midst of this attack I knew it was important for someone to witness what was happening. Red dashed across the porch, leaped over the banister, and took aim with his rifle. I hollered, "Don't shoot him, Red!" and stood between the two with my arms outstretched. By this time the guy had jumped into his car and was screeching off. Mrs. Boynton rushed me to the hospital. Dr. Dinkins, son of Dr. William Dinkins, patched me up with seven stitches. How I survived, I don't know. I was very lucky that night.

During the vicious attack I had a warm feeling under my skin that came over me from my head and traveled down my entire body. I believe that it was a spiritual empowerment that allowed me to feel an extraordinary sense of internal strength instead of fear. I felt an intense force that seemed to lift me up emotionally, even though I didn't know what would happen next. It was a surrendering of life, in a sense, and I was prepared. This surreal feeling happened to me only twice in my life, both times when I was physically attacked. I view it as a form of resistance, with support from a power beyond myself.

Unfortunately, the meaning of nonviolence to many people is that when you get hit on one cheek, you turn the other cheek and you don't do anything. However, nonviolence really means fighting back with another purpose and with other nonviolent weapons. The fight is to win that person over, a struggle of the human spirit, much more challenging than fisticuffs.

One of the reasons people attack you is that they have already reduced your humanity and view you as an object. Looking directly at an attacker, eye to eye, reinforces the idea that you are a human being and that he or she, too, is a human being with choices. You can disarm someone to a certain extent by a nonviolent response, because it is unexpected behavior. I'm sure the attacker was a bit surprised when I continued to get up and face him without striking back or defending myself, refusing to succumb. I didn't know at the beginning that he had a gun and was planning to kill me. However, I am aware that Red's gun may have saved my life.

Or perhaps it was just having a witness there. I can only hope that when those two men reflected about the incident that night they perhaps were changed in some small way. Maybe the attacker would remember that I looked him in the eye as he bashed my skull. Maybe he would remember I told Red not to shoot him. Maybe someday he will be glad that he didn't pull the trigger and kill me. Maybe.

Colia was in Jackson, Mississippi, at that time and had been working with Medgar and actively involved in the NAACP. When she heard about Medgar, she tried to telephone me to let me know what had happened. She was unable to reach me because I was in the hospital being sewn up from my attack at approximately the same time Medgar was killed. I didn't hear about his death until the next day.

I learned later about the tri-state conspiracy from the FBI. Edwin R. Tully was the FBI special agent from Mobile in charge of investigating my attack. He investigated because I was a voter registration worker and there was a Department of Justice injunction in Selma. My attackers were never found. A state legislator, Byron De La Beckwith, was arrested for Medgar's murder, but two trials in 1964 ended with hung juries. However, thirty years later, in 1994, it was determined that he had bragged about killing Medgar, and he was convicted in a new trial.[1]

There had been a number of attacks on civil rights leaders throughout the South over the years. When we took the leadership, particularly staff positions, we recognized that we were putting our lives on the line by simply holding a title. It was common to get death threats. I never knew from one day to the next what might befall me.

The feelings of blacks in Selma toward me changed after that night because they realized I was prepared to give my life for a cause that would serve them. There was a different climate, a new attitude. People not only sympathized; they offered genuine support. After this incident more people attended mass meetings and voter registration classes, and committed to attempting to register at the courthouse.

For several days I wore the stained, bloody shirt I had been wearing during the attack. It roused the conscience of the community and became a personal flyer and billboard that emphasized the importance of registering to vote. When I think about this incident, I remember Medgar. I can still imagine his family seeing him in a pool of blood on the floor of his carport with his wife trying to shield the children from the tragic scene. As I reflect about the entire night, it was not just about me. I survived. Ben Cox survived. My friend Medgar didn't.

While the motive on the part of those who perpetrated violence was to discourage us, our response to the violence was the opposite. These assassinations and attacks awakened people and shook them into realizing new meaning to life. I believe that the value of life lies not in longevity but in what people do to give significance. Rather than focus on the length of our physical lives, we turned internally and determined the measure of our lives in terms of what could be done to serve others that could give our lives deeper meaning. This is how life is expanded—it's not just your space in time but your experiences in the minds of others that give it longevity and importance. I wanted to become an example for others to follow, learning early that life is more than simply breathing.

When the number of people at the voter registration office increased and the lines got longer, registration attempts were met with increased resistance from Sheriff Jim Clark. Often when registrants were waiting their turn, a deputy blocked the door, or they were harassed. When the lines stretched down the hall and out the door onto the front steps of the courthouse, Sheriff Clark ordered those in line to leave. They refused, and this began a new phase of the campaign as dozens, then hundreds, of registrants were arrested. We liked that the jails were filling up and it was overloading the system. The county had to provide food for everyone, which was costly. For every jailed individual, paperwork had to be processed, bond money had to be posted, and a court date had to be set. Each and every person put in jail had to appear in court, which overwhelmed the court system. Additional staff were not employed to handle large numbers of registrants, so the process was slowed down.

Throughout the summer of 1963, as the number of adults who were prepared to go to jail was dwindling, the youth stepped up, eager to be involved directly. The issue of allowing teenagers to be involved was discussed, and it was somewhat controversial. The adult leaders agreed that the young people should be allowed to participate if they wanted to, but we were still fearful of them being injured. We realized, though, that they would be the ones to benefit the most from the change we were working toward. This was part of their education, learning how to stand up for their rights and suffer if necessary to gain and keep their rights. It was essential for them to learn the strategies of nonviolence.

On a regular basis we organized marches. The youth wanted to march and go to jail in large numbers. I don't think we could have stopped them even if we had tried. They were young, energetic, and committed. They knew that they could have an impact without the fear of losing jobs, like their parents would, because they were too young to work. Going to jail for a moral cause was a badge of honor rather than a blight on their record. Although our focus was voter registration, we had to exercise our First Amendment right, freedom of speech. Dr. King said that we have to "fight for the right to fight for our rights."

It was necessary to sustain the action because it often proved to be an opportunity for people to participate. Invariably, with each march there were new people who hadn't marched before. Some had family members and friends who had marched and gone to jail and they didn't want to miss the chance to share that same experience. In some cases the young people thought they might get left out and demanded that we organize a march so that they could "exercise their rights." It was common to hear people comment, "When are we going to have another march?" Some had been arrested before and had regrouped, ready to go to jail the second, third, and even fourth time. Jail had been used as a threat to those attempting to gain their rights. However, pride, satisfaction, and self-respect glowed on their faces as they held their heads high, stuck their chests out, and presented themselves to be arrested. Their willingness to suffer became a transforming power and a new way of thinking that overcame the barriers that attempted to force them back in their "places." This barrier had now been removed. Adults were inspired by the young people's acts of courage and pursued the same course of action. I don't recall any incidents of violence during these marches and arrests. People were truly learning to be nonviolent, not striking back. Like a running back who gets tackled on the ten-yard line, they felt that it would not be long before they made the goal. We were getting closer.

Throughout the months a number of national leaders came to Selma to join with local leaders and show their support. For one of the marches, Rev. C. T. Vivian and some local ministers joined together at the courthouse, lined up, and challenged the city's efforts of discouragement to register. Rev. Vivian had been my homiletics teacher at American Baptist Theological Seminary in Nashville. He always worked very closely with the students, and he not only encouraged us but joined us on the front line of the marches and even in jail, where we once shared a cell. When the jailer came to release us, we were exchanging puns and enjoying each other's wit, so we told the jailer to wait until we finished. The jailer couldn't believe it. A persuasive speaker, Rev. Vivian drove his points home with such riveting force that people were knocked off their feet. And here he was again, back on the front line, still outspoken, ever ready to take a stand for what is right.

On this day, Sheriff Clark and his deputies began to push back the registrants away from the door. Rev. Vivian was struck with a billy club and shoved down the steps. There was an exchange between him and the sheriff. Rev. Vivian verbally protested to the sheriff that he was denying people the right to vote by blocking them at the courthouse door. Sheriff Clark looked down the line, studying the faces, and claimed that several had felony convictions. Rev. Vivian said that Sheriff Clark was the one who made them felons, that they should be allowed to come and register, and that if they were felons, that would be determined in the process. At that point Rev. Vivian was struck on the head and thrust back, but he said, "You can arrest us, but don't beat us on the street."

Alabama had already experienced success with the Montgomery Bus Boycott in 1955 and in Birmingham in May 1963. It was not uncommon to see law enforcement officers and politicians wearing buttons that said, "NEVER!" I got the impression they were sending a message to whites in Alabama, which emphatically stated, "You let the blacks integrate in Montgomery and Birmingham, but in Dallas County—NEVER." Sheriff Jim Clark proudly displayed this button on his uniform to prove a point. Often when people or communities feel inferior they overcompensate by using excessive force to dominate those who they feel are weaker. Or in this case, they sent a strong message about their feelings without even opening their mouths.

Father Maurice Ouellet was the white Catholic priest at St. Elizabeth's Mission in Selma. This was a compound that included a church, a school, and a hospital that served the black community. The church was next door to the Tabernacle Baptist Church. Father Ouellet used the educational facilities at night for training the youth and planning for the ongoing sit-ins downtown. He had moved to Selma from New England, and although an outsider, he was respected by both the black and white communities. Father Ouellet and I occasionally met at night, and he shared with me some of the thoughts and opinions of the white business people in town. As administrator of the school, hospital, and church, he dealt with many of the white businessmen. We held many mass meetings but he had never attended.

One night Father Ouellet told me, "I've been thinking long and hard about something and wanted to talk with you about it. My church members and schoolchildren are black, and I want to attend a mass meeting to support them. What do you think?" Until that point no local whites had shown any interest in attending the meetings, except the law enforcement officials.

I said, "Your position in Selma will change once you make that commitment. Many white people will no longer trust you, they may cut off communication with you, and it may affect your relationship with the Catholic Church and your business dealings, as well. Ponder this before you make a decision, as it will thrust you into a lonely world." I felt that it was only fair for him to be aware of how that decision would change his life. Every night we met he kept asking what I thought he should do and I refused to advise him. I always said, "Follow your conscience." We prayed, two ministers together, seeking higher answers.

Finally, he said, "Bernard, I've made up my mind. I'm going to attend a mass meeting." He wanted to show that the movement was not only supported by blacks.

My response was, "If you're coming, let's make it official and have you be the keynote speaker for the evening." He accepted and became the first white speaker at our mass meetings. Father Ouellet represented the whites of goodwill, maybe even some of the local whites in Selma who didn't have the courage to speak out. He gave a powerful and conscience-provoking talk. At the end of the meeting we all joined hands, right over left in our traditional way, and sang "We Shall Overcome," swaying back and forth as one body.

The next day the front page of the *Selma Times Journal* displayed a photograph of Father Ouellet with arms crossed, holding hands with a black woman. The caption read "White Priest dances with Negro woman at Mass Meeting." That was an erroneous interpretation. Even though the article was hurtful, Father Ouellet was proud that he had spoken his convictions and had taken an admirable stand. He received a very positive response, particularly from his black congregation, demonstrating what real leadership was. His commitment encouraged his parishioners to get involved and to attempt to register to vote. He lived out his own Christian principles by putting his deep beliefs into practice. I considered it a breakthrough in broadening the campaign. He had broken the chain of fear for many of the whites and blacks in Selma who believed in this cause but were concerned about the negative consequences of acting on their beliefs. However, this stance of support was not without heavy cost to the priest. He incurred the wrath of a number of white community members, which created some problems between him and the Catholic Church. He even received death threats. Because Father Ouellet was an outspoken advocate of racial justice and spoke against unfair, vicious tactics used by the police, Archbishop Thomas Toolen eventually transferred him from Selma to Mystic, Connecticut.[2]

I'm certain that Father Ouellet's bold move to attend mass meetings gave other white individuals the courage to stand up for a cause they knew was right. It was a weighty move that showed his internal strength and helped us to branch out in new directions, seeking more support from the white community. Dr. King talked with us many times about the conditions necessary to bring about change, or revolution. One of those prerequisites was the need for the sympathy, if not the active support, of the majority. The majority cannot be simply numerical, but those in power. Therefore, our appeal in the nonviolence movement had always included soliciting active support and sympathy from those who represented the majority. White organizations, churches, and labor unions were constantly in Dr. King's scope when he looked at support areas. Although blacks primarily were the ones who were denied the right to vote in a systematic way, the entire nation was affected. As Dr. King stated, "Injustice anywhere is a threat to justice everywhere."[3]

Selma was an important experiment because there were various forces operating. One central force was the church, not just in Selma but throughout the country, giving its members constant sustenance. There was a surprising show of support by a group from the white Alabama churches who called themselves Concerned White Citizens of Alabama. About twenty-five members came to me, and spokesman Jim McPherson said, "We want to march in support of your voter registration for blacks. But we will only include white marchers." I was never quite sure why they didn't want blacks to march with them, but I figured that they wanted to make a statement and be clear that they were taking this stand alone. My guess was that there was a tacit agreement between these local white marchers and the sheriff's office to march peacefully.

On the day of the planned march, they drove into downtown Selma and parked their cars on the curb. They gathered at Knox Reformed Presbyterian Church, which was their base headquarters. This group marched in silence down the street about a block and ended at Brown Chapel. Then they turned around and marched back into the center of town, got in their cars, and drove away. It probably took longer to plan and organize than to actually march. I think it satisfied their consciences, though, that as a group they had taken some action representing the white church of Alabama. It was a curious and strange event, but we appreciated their support. Maybe this was their answer to King's call to affirm their belief in the cause and to show that all whites were not opposed to the voting rights initiative.

When the numbers began to wane for applicants to attempt to vote in Selma, we decided to branch out into the surrounding regions of Dallas County. We selected Bogue Chitto, a black community that sat on a tract of land covering about six thousand acres and that was mostly owned and farmed by black residents who were descendants of slaves. Although the residents weren't well educated, they were proud to own their farms and were strongly independent. However, they stayed to themselves. This community was known around the state as "Freetown," and the residents worked together to improve their community. When we asked if they wanted to register to vote, they responded with an enthusiastic yes. Although many of the people from that area couldn't read or write, they could answer the questions orally. The government was required to accommodate them, so they took oral exams and marked their signatures with an X. It was funny how the more sophisticated people in Selma were spurred on to go down and register, not wanting the Bogue Chitto residents to get one up on them.

Sometimes we received requests in the oddest situations. A white farmer in Dallas County surprised me by asking for assistance. He said, "Bernard, can you help the Negroes on my farm get registered to vote?"

I said, "Sure, I'll help," wondering why he was so interested.

I sent over a team who helped the workers learn how to fill out the application form and practice answering sample questions on the literacy tests. Later, I learned that his son who was away at college was returning and was planning to run for political office in the county. The farmer wanted to get votes for his son. There were about fifty black workers on his farm who would certainly vote for the son since his father employed them and helped them get registered to vote. When the white farmer took truckloads of his laborers into the courthouse to register, every single one of them passed. Some signed an X on the form because they couldn't read or write. Although the farmer had an ulterior motive, it worked for us, too. We always liked it when there was a reciprocal relationship. He thanked me for preparing them. It was clear that because a white man vouched for the laborers and brought them in himself, the registrar passed them whether they answered the test correctly or not. Whatever the reason, I was happy that a large group was now registered to vote.

Next I turned my efforts toward voter registration in Wilcox County, which also had a large number of black families. Although we had some rough encounters with Sheriff Jim Clark in Dallas County, I soon found out that the sheriff in Wilcox County was even more obstinate. Sheriff P. C. "Lummie" Jenkins was known throughout the county as being mean to the core. He was a tall man with a long rectangular face, a square jaw, and a cleft chin. Usually dressed in a coat and tie, he wore his hat pulled down to his eyebrows, shading his spectacled eyes. From his thin lips spewed hateful words.

In these remote southern counties the sheriffs were actually the lords of the territory. They ruled everything and had the ability to recruit posses when they needed more manpower to look for fugitives or suspects. Sheriffs had control over commerce in the area, particularly contraband, such as the sale of moonshine or weapons. In fact, they used to be referred to as "the Law" because whatever they said was the law, no matter what was actually legal. Sheriffs had a sense of ownership of the land and people, which the residents of the county respected out of fear.

An account was passed down in Wilcox County that Sheriff Jenkins went to a black woman's house asking the whereabouts of her son. When he questioned her, she gave no response, which he took as an insult and a sign of disrespect. He was convinced that she knew where her son was and was refusing to tell him. Unbeknownst to him, she was unable to speak owing to a stroke that had paralyzed her, and she was confined to a wheelchair. The sheriff slapped her several times with such force that she later had a heart attack and died. Nothing was done about the incident.

In the rural areas Mr. Gildersleeve (one of the "Courageous Eight") made the contact for me in Wilcox County, and the two of us met privately in homes with no more than five or six people, trying to keep a low profile and not call attention to ourselves. Mr. Gildersleeve was a teacher at the Lutheran Academy, an all-black, independent, private high school in Selma. He had a strong presence and represented leadership in the community.

We didn't want Sheriff Jenkins or anyone else getting suspicious and interfering with our work. We went to a part of the county called Boykins, also known as Gee's Bend, which is famous for its handmade quilts. The area got its name from the way the slaves had plowed the land in the river bend—when they pulled the mules to turn left or right they called out "gee" or "haw." The Alabama River winds an almost circle around the region that created an eight-by-sixteen-mile peninsula. It was so isolated that the area remained much the same in the twentieth century as it had been more than one hundred years before. During the Great Depression, the Gee's Bend residents nearly starved to death. The Red Cross sent desperately needed aid to the inhabitants of that remote area, an experience that had a profound impact on the outlook of the residents in the Bend continuing into the following decades.[4]

Originally this area had been a plantation owned by a Mr. Pettway. When he died, the Tuskegee Institute received a federal government grant to go into Gee's Bend and help the people there maintain their livelihood. The plantation was divided into lots, and each family was able to purchase a small slice of the land with the assistance of low-interest rates from the federal government. Eventually they built a school there. The government farm agents gave them washing machines and assistance that led the black families to becoming independent and self-sufficient.

Because they had benefited from the federal program, most felt a sense of citizenship and national community, even if they didn't feel connected to the rest of the county.

I think this isolated group of individuals was able to organize and stand up against racial repression because it was already a close-knit community. Families depended on each other, and many of the families were related by birth or marriage. They worked together and shared everything like one large extended family. Another reason they were able to stand up for what was right in their county was that they were landowners and were not subject to the economic intimidation that sharecroppers had to suffer. I knew that if we could get the leader to agree to having us come in and help them learn about the voter registration process, the entire community would agree.

For several weeks we prepared them to fill out the voter registration forms, instructed them how to answer the literacy test, and trained them to help others. As an organizer, it is necessary to identify people who can connect you to others, similar to attaching one quilt piece to another. Eventually, when more pieces are sewn together, a broad area is covered, like a full-size quilt. We worked piece by piece until every eligible person in Gee's Bend was trained. Alex Brown, the high school student from Birmingham who came to work with us in Selma, was left in Gee's Bend to continue this work since he had relatives there.

When I thought the families were ready, I planned to take a select group to the county seat of Camden, to attempt to register. The night before we went to the courthouse, a decision had to be made about which family members would go and which ones would stay. We didn't know what kind of trouble awaited us, or what our fate would be, so the decision was made to take just one member of each family. The families decided that only men would go, even though the women were also well prepared. It was especially difficult for men to remain nonviolent, as they might have to watch the women being beaten and yet refrain from fighting to protect them. We gained a lot of respect for the women because of their internal strength and commitment. Everyone was aware that it was a perilous situation and that under no circumstances would I allow guns to be taken. Some men were not comfortable without their guns, as guns were their way of life. Carrying a gun for them was like carrying a wallet. They felt like they weren't fully dressed without one. Some excluded themselves from going because they refused to go without a gun. The rest assured me that they would go unarmed.

We wanted to let the people decide what they were ready to do, because in the past they had been left out of the decision making. We presented information about the voting process and assisted them in getting prepared, but most important, we allowed them to take the leadership. It was a problem, however, when we wanted to turn the leadership over to them and they didn't want to do it nonviolently.

The humorous thing was that the husbands had to tell their wives where their money was hidden. Because they didn't trust the banks, the men stashed their money in different places around the house, like a private savings account. The women were very happy to finally know where the money was.

Our goal was to accompany one group from Gee's Bend in to register to vote, and then turn over the leadership role to others in the county to go with them for the next registrations. This was the only group I ever took to register, and I went mainly because it was so dangerous and I wanted to be with them in case an incident occurred. I assured them that without weapons we could achieve the goals we were trying to reach. They were used to registering their cars and their guns, but they had never attempted to register themselves. My strategy was to get them started, to overcome the first barrier—fear of what might happen. Sometimes the only thing needed is to help individuals take that first step. Monroe Pettway, the leader of the Gee's Bend group, brought the community together, organized them, and presented the proposal that they go as a group to register to vote. I didn't want them to be dependent on me; rather, I wanted them to find good leadership and to work to support each other. I was willing to get them started, to show it can happen peacefully, and then leave it up to them to continue. If they were refused, I would be there to show that the county was interfering with their efforts to register to vote, therefore violating the federal injunction prohibiting anyone from interfering with any black person's right to vote. I had to anticipate this action, but I was hopeful they would be allowed to exercise their right to register.

On a Thursday morning in 1963, our group of anxious applicants walked into the Wilcox County Courthouse. We knew they were expecting us at the registrar's office since we had notified them we were coming, but a sign posted on the door said, "CLOSED." It was supposed to be open because it was the right day and the right time. The hallway was lined with straight, hard wooden benches, where we sat facing the closed door, waiting. It was quiet. Eerily quiet.

Some of the clerks came by and looked at us. Occasionally someone would come out and say, "The office isn't open yet," or "This person went to lunch," or "That person is on break." We told them that we would just sit and wait. We waited. And waited. I admired the patience and boldness of the black men sitting there in their own county. This was a huge step for them since no black individual had even attempted to register in more than fifty years.

We sat there for about two hours. As we waited, one question we discussed was how long we should we stay. The media were outside. The day before we had called the *New York Times,* the *Los Angeles Times,* the *Washington Post,* the Associated Press, and UPI Wire Services because of their wide readerships. In addition we had informed the U.S. Department of Justice in Washington, the local state unit of the FBI, and, last, the local law enforcement. The federal government was quick to respond because of the injunction prohibiting interference with any black person's right to vote. They all continued to wait and see what was going to happen. At some point the courthouse was going to close for the day. In planning, we intended to just test the system; it was not a protest. If the applicants were allowed to register, then there would be no problem and no need to go further. Wilcox County did not want to be in the limelight or create problems for the Department of Justice. They wanted to avoid any kind of confrontation. Eventually it turned out that the people from the Department of Justice had planned to use this occasion as the basis of a suit for denying people the right to vote.

At 3:00 P.M. the door finally opened and the men filed in one by one. Each person completed the application form and took the literacy test that they had practiced several times. The paper and pencil exam took about thirty to forty-five minutes. Some of the men signed their application with an X because they couldn't write. Some took oral exams. As registrants finished, they went outside and waited. The press was there and interviewed me, as a SNCC worker. But there was little fanfare. We got into our cars and trucks and drove away, being careful to watch the speed limit. We went to the church to celebrate. "Nothin' to it," many said. Once this first group made the bold step to register, it was open for everyone. Each applicant was supposed to get a voting card in the mail in about a month, giving them their official right to vote if they passed. And sure enough, a month later, the voter registration cards arrived for every single one of them. As an organizer I felt that this was a successful mission. I had walked with them to take the first step together and supported them. Now they were ready to walk alone, but with support from each other.

One barrier for people registering to vote was fear of what would happen to them or their families. Being successful in registering helped them to take a huge mental leap to overcome that fear. They had to anticipate how they would respond if the situation turned violent. We armed them with nonviolent responses, without their guns, and equipped them with self-confidence and strength of spirit. The other barrier was apprehension of failing the literacy test. However, by preparing for the tests, they overcame their worry and became bold. One mission was complete.

Many years later, when I went back to Selma for the annual celebration of the Bloody Sunday March, I visited Mr. Gildersleeve. I asked him a question that had been nagging me for years: "Mr. Gildersleeve, remember that time you drove me in your car to Wilcox County to Lonnie Brown's house to a voter registration meeting? We agreed that no one would take a gun. I had a suspicious feeling that you carried a gun. I just want to know, now tell me the truth, did you have your gun with you that day?"

He thought a minute, looked up to the ceiling, then down at the floor, avoiding my eyes. He fidgeted around awhile and then looked straight at me, grinned a little, and said, "Yeah, I believe I did have a gun. I carried it along just in case we needed it. I didn't want to shoot anybody, but I thought we might need it to scare people off." We had a big laugh. I just shook my head. He could have gotten us and others killed by carrying a weapon. The leaders of SNCC were struggling with the issue of local people carrying guns, which was completely opposed to our nonviolent methods. Even though we understood their position and didn't want to impose our values on them, we couldn't afford to have weapons brought into our activities. On that we held firm.

Rev. Lonnie Brown was a young insurance agent from Wilcox County who sold insurance to the black community. He was a leader in the community and helped train people to take the literacy test. Many of the blacks were sharecroppers, and Lonnie wasn't allowed to go across the land to get to their houses. He had to get special permission from the white landowners to go onto their property. He took a big risk in identifying with this movement because he could, and probably did, lose business from his connection with us. Some meetings for test preparation were held at his house, and I knew then he was not afraid. It was people like Rev. Lonnie Brown who inspired me.

One night I was driving back from Wilcox County alone, and three vehicles were blocking the road ahead. It looked like trouble, so I had to decide whether to turn around and go back to safety, swerve off the side of the road around them, or just pull up to them and stop. I decided that if it was my time to go, then I'd just take my chances. I slowed down, stopped, and waited as three men approached me. An old man aimed a double-barrel shotgun straight at my head, his hands shaking. He looked at me and said, "Hey, are you the one who can't say 'yes sir' and 'no sir'?"

I told him, "I don't have any problem with those words. I can say them just fine." I turned and stared straight into the muzzle of his shotgun and said, "Yes sir, no sir, yes sir, no sir." They all stood there in silence looking at each other, then at me. I was worried that his shaky hands would hit the trigger. Finally, the old man lowered the gun and the three of them walked back to their trucks, got in, and drove away.

I could actually imagine my brain being spattered against the windows. There were several incidents I experienced where I thought my life was over. This was one of them. I couldn't believe it when the men turned away and left. How was I still alive? Once they walked to their cars I felt a rush of relief. Certainly, this was an answered prayer.

I decided right then and there never to go again to Wilcox County by myself. For the longest time I was puzzled about why they stopped me and why they kept asking about the "yes sir, no sir" questions. It seemed so odd. Finally I figured out that it all came out of a court case where I was a witness for the Justice Department suit that was filed against Dallas

County. While I was under cross-examination, Defense Attorney McLean Pitts asked me a question, and when I answered, he objected that I didn't say, "Yes, sir." The prosecuting attorney from the Justice Department, John Doar, stood at the back of the room and boomed loud and clear, "Rev. LaFayette answered the question. It's not required that he respond with 'sir.'" I'm sure that old man with the shotgun must have been in the courtroom that day, remembered that incident, and decided to act on it. But out of context, he couldn't identify me. I was lucky that they didn't just shoot me anyway.

There's a difference between being courageous and being radical and confrontational. The question should always be, "Is this particular action going to move you closer to your cause, or is it an unnecessary risk?" I was prepared to give my life; therefore they couldn't take it from me. Even though I wasn't afraid, I also didn't want to provoke their erratic behavior. The old man was expecting me to deny it when he asked, "Are you the one?" and to respond, "No, it wasn't me," and then they would have been satisfied that I *was* the one. I believe that it was my unusual action in an extreme situation that made them question their assumption. For those who practice nonviolence, it's not necessary to court death. If it comes in the course of your action, let it be. You must restrain your behavior and make sure that you aren't overreacting, but rather responding in a creative way to achieve your goal. Stay focused on your goal. Don't invite violence. But face it when necessary.

It was people like Attorney Doar who made my life much easier in Selma. It's hard to calculate John Doar's value to the civil rights movement, as he was involved in many high-profile cases throughout the 1960s and was a huge champion for our cause. Bright and articulate, he held degrees from Princeton University and the University of California, Berkeley. Working through the Department of Justice, he was the assistant attorney general for civil rights and was one of the contributors to the Civil Rights Act of 1964. Whenever he was around, we felt the presence of the federal government, which was one of our goals—to get the federal government to take action to protect our rights as United States citizens. In most cases, Attorney Doar was the one and only person who represented the federal government. He stood tall physically and morally and gave us the confidence that a good "big brother" was watching us.

Rozelia Forrester ("Ma Foster"), Bernard LaFayette Jr.'s grandmother (Personal collection of B. LaFayette Jr.)

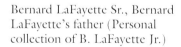

Bernard LaFayette Sr., Bernard LaFayette's father (Personal collection of B. LaFayette Jr.)

Verdell LaFayette, Bernard LaFayette Jr.'s mother (Personal collection of B. LaFayette Jr.)

Bernard LaFayette Jr. around age seven, known as "Little Man" in the church (Personal collection of B. LaFayette Jr.)

Bernard LaFayette Jr.'s sisters and mother (top row, left to right: Geraldine Coverson, Victoria Wanda Davis, Brenda Austin; bottom row, left to right: Joyce Davis Wright, Verdell LaFayette, Rozelia Kennedy) (Personal collection of B. LaFayette Jr.)

Kate LaFayette, Bernard's wife (Personal collection of B. LaFayette Jr.)

Bernard LaFayette Jr. (standing, right) with Michael Anthony
LaFayette, his brother (standing, left), and Bernard LaFayette Sr., his
father (seated) (Personal collection of B. LaFayette Jr.)

(Above) Front row, left to right: C. T. Vivian, Diane Nash, Bernard LaFayette Jr. at Nashville march (Personal collection of B. LaFayette Jr.) *(Below)* First Baptist Church, Selma (K. L. Johnson)

Bernard LaFayette Jr. (left) and James Lawson, nonviolence teacher in Nashville (Personal collection of B. LaFayette Jr.)

(Above) Brown Chapel AME Church, Selma (Courtesy of the National Voting Rights Museum and Institute) *(Below)* Tabernacle Baptist Church (Courtesy of the National Voting Rights Museum and Institute)

Bernard LaFayette Jr.'s driver's license from Selma (Personal collection of B. LaFayette Jr.)

Amelia Boynton, Courageous Eight (Courtesy of the National Voting Rights Museum and Institute)

Ernest Doyle, Courageous Eight (Courtesy of the National Voting Rights Museum and Institute)

Rev. Frederick Reese, Courageous Eight (Courtesy of the National Voting Rights Museum and Institute)

Rev. H. Shannon,
Courageous Eight (Courtesy
of the National Voting Rights
Museum and Institute)

James E. Gildersleeve,
Courageous Eight (Courtesy
of the National Voting Rights
Museum and Institute)

Marie Foster, Courageous
Eight (Courtesy of the
National Voting Rights
Museum and Institute)

Boise Reese (Personal
collection of B. LaFayette Jr.)

Rev. J. D. Hunter, Courageous Eight (Courtesy of the National Voting Rights Museum and Institute)

Ulysses Blackmon, Courageous Eight (Courtesy of the National Voting Rights Museum and Institute)

Rev. Lewis Lloyd Anderson (Courtesy of the National Voting Rights Museum and Institute)

Bernard LaFayette Jr. after an attempted assassination by the Ku Klux Klan, Selma (Personal collection of B. LaFayette Jr.)

Andrew Young (left), Dr. King (second from left), and James Orange (center) at a rally in Selma (Courtesy of the National Voting Rights Museum and Institute)

Lois Reeves at mass meeting at First Baptist Church, Selma (Personal collection of B. LaFayette Jr.)

(Above) James Bevel (second from left) (Courtesy of the National Voting Rights Museum and Institute) *(Below)* Dallas County Courthouse (Courtesy of the National Voting Rights Museum and Institute)

Sixteenth Street Baptist Church, Birmingham (K. L. Johnson)

(Above) Dr. King speaking in front of Brown Chapel, Selma (Courtesy of the National Voting Rights Museum and Institute) *(Below)* Andrew Young (standing left) at a rally in Selma, crossing the Edmund Pettus Bridge (Courtesy of the National Voting Rights Museum and Institute)

Dr. King and Bernard LaFayette Jr. (Personal collection of B. LaFayette Jr.)

Edmund Pettus
Bridge, Selma
(K. L. Johnson)

Selma as viewed from the bridge (K. L. Johnson)

State capitol in Montgomery on the final day of the Selma to Montgomery March (Courtesy of the National Voting Rights Museum and Institute)

(Above) John Lewis, Fred Shuttlesworth, and Bernard LaFayette Jr. at reenactment of the Selma to Montgomery March, Montgomery (Personal collection of B. LaFayette Jr.) *(Below)* Highway 80, where Viola Liuzzo was killed (K. L. Johnson)

Bernard LaFayette Jr. at the National Voting Rights Museum in Selma, standing in front of two photographs from 1963: one a mug shot from his arrest, the other from when he was attacked in Selma. (P. H. Zappardino)

5

Mountains and Valleys

Good actions give strength to ourselves and inspire good actions in others.

—Plato

During this period in our history of the struggle, overlapping with my time in Selma, there were other movements in effect throughout the country. There was a hopeful atmosphere, a cloud of despair had been pierced, and movement was in the air. Popular artists wrote or performed songs that embraced the themes of the movement, making "protest" songs part of the widespread culture. Some of these were Bob Dylan's "Blowin' in the Wind" and "The Times They Are a-Changin'," the Byrds' "Turn, Turn, Turn," Phil Ochs's "Here's to the State of Mississippi" and "The Ballad of Medgar Evers," the Buffalo Springfield's "For What It's Worth," Sam Cooke's "A Change Is Gonna Come," and the civil rights anthem "We Shall Overcome," popularized by Guy Carawan and Joan Baez. These and countless more protest songs were performed all over the world at concerts and music festivals and were played on the radio. Most young people knew these songs and artists. Music gets into the fabric of our souls and helps to shape our beliefs.

The cry for "One man, one vote" was echoed in places such as Africa. Activists were moving from one movement to another, transporting the spirit. Struggles were coming to the forefront, and the personalities of the leaders were buoyed by the media coverage, bringing their plights to light. Rather than these movements of human rights and liberation being sequenced or parallel, they converged, blending into each other. The mid-1960s held much promise not just in our country but also around the world. Other countries that were under colonial rule were throwing off shackles and winning independence, and many political prisoners were being released from jail. Freedom was beginning to ring in the East African countries of Tanzania (April 26, 1964), Zambia (October 24, 1964), and Zimbabwe (November 11, 1965), and in Gambia in West Africa (February 18, 1965).[1]

A historic day for the civil rights movement was August 28, 1963, when the long-planned and well-organized March on Washington marched onto television sets in every household in America, more than 200,000 people strong. The goals of the march were jobs and freedom. In addition, the focus was on desegregation of public accommodations and public schools, protection for the right to vote, barring of employment discrimination, and economic justice. The march was organized by Bayard Rustin, one of the longtime leaders in the civil rights movement, and A. Philip Randolph of the Pullman Car Porters Union.

The highlight of the event was when Dr. King took the podium as the final speaker of the afternoon and delivered his famous "I Have a Dream" speech, which spoke to the hearts of not just black America but most all America. The importance of this event to the entire civil rights movement can never be overstated; I think it could be considered the high point. Afterward, Dr. King and other leaders of the march met with President Kennedy and Vice President Johnson and began to lay out the framework for the Civil Rights Act.

I went back and forth in my mind about whether or not to go to the march. Someone in a leadership position needed to be on hand in Alabama to deal with any problems that might occur in response to the march. So after a discussion of the situation with SNCC members and the local leaders in Selma, a decision was made for one of us to remain in Alabama in case there was any backlash from this national and historic event. And that someone was me. We were so proud, though, to fill a couple of chartered buses going to Washington, D.C., representing the Selma community. I was apprehensive, especially about a march of that magnitude, fearful that somebody might try to sabotage it. I felt so elated when it was peaceful. It was a great day of celebration. The American spirit came forth strong, as it became clear that many people from across the entire country of all cultures, nationalities, religions, and ages supported the movement. Thankfully, everything was quiet in Selma the day of the march and the following days. While in Selma, we were trying to change not only the town but the nation to say, "No, we will not accept these conditions," Dr. King said, "Whatever affects one directly affects all indirectly."[2]

Later on I had several conversations with fellow SNCC workers who were there that day in Washington, D.C., and I learned about the controversy over John Lewis's speech. The twenty-three-year-old SNCC chairman was the youngest of the speakers for this event. He wanted the speech to represent SNCC's position on the hard issues of the civil rights movement, to bring fire and spirit into his words. He later told me that he wanted his speech to move beyond just the support of the pending civil rights bill and to go more deeply into the heart of the critical problems that black Americans had experienced for years. To do that he felt it necessary to choose carefully words that would reflect a tone of frustration and impatience. His speech originally contained a military metaphor of General Sherman's march through Dixie in the Civil War, which implied that blacks might be incited to march through the South in a not-so-peaceful way. Other critical remarks about President Kennedy's bill being "too little, too late," and stinging phrases such as "cheap political leaders," raised serious concerns. Critical feedback had been received from SCLC leaders and March on Washington coordinators, as well as from Archbishop Patrick O'Boyle and Attorney General Robert Kennedy, who all wanted John to tone down the negative and military rhetoric. John argued to keep his speech exactly as he had written it, but others pushed him to make it less offensive. The program had already begun with speakers addressing the crowd from the podium on the steps of the Lincoln Memorial. As speeches were being delivered in front of Abraham Lincoln's statue, heated arguments were taking place behind the statue to persuade John to alter his text. At the very last minute, just when it looked as if neither side would give in, A. Philip Randolph looked John in the eye and said simply, "We've come this far together. Let us *stay* together." With that plea, John quickly reworked his speech to make it less confrontational, yet kept intact what he considered the strong content of his message.[3] I thought it was a great speech, but I agreed that the last-minute revisions he made were the right thing to do in keeping unity in the movement. After all, the purpose of the march was to support jobs and freedom, which are nonmilitant. I believe that nonviolence should be assertive without being aggressive. John's speech went down in history as one of the most powerful and memorable speeches of this event.

When the march ended and the buses rolled back home, my friends who were at the march shared their enthusiasm, telling me every detail of the event. The big talk was about Dr. King's speech, the brilliance of his words. All were amazed at the size of the crowd and jubilant that it was nonviolent.

Although I would like to have attended this landmark event, I have no regrets about not being there. My attitude has always been to serve wherever I was most needed. If I could fulfill the purpose by remaining in Selma "on call," in case of emergency, then I wanted to do my job. I like to give leadership when needed, but I don't always have to be out front. Working behind the scenes is important work, too.

After watching Dr. King's speech on television, I was very much convinced that things would never be the same. First, it was an opportunity for the whole nation and entire world to hear his message for the first time in its entirety, not just short statements in a newscast. I thought from this point on that people would have a more positive attitude about the changes he was demanding. Second, I was impressed with the large number of whites who were there. I kept hearing Dr. King's voice in my mind saying how important it was to win the sympathy of the majority. When I saw the throng of white faces, adults and children, I was elated. Third, I was amazed that all of this was happening right in the middle of our nation's capital on the steps of the Lincoln Memorial.

Although I didn't really get a clear sense of what the white people of Selma thought or how they felt about the March on Washington, I was pleased that there was no immediate reaction from Sheriff Clark. That momentous event seemed to be a turning point that gave impetus to the people of Selma. Dr. King had even referred to Alabama in his speech: "I have a dream that one day, down in Alabama, with its vicious racists, with its governor having his lips dripping with the words of interposition and nullification; one day right there in Alabama, little black boys and black girls will be able to join hands with little white boys and white girls as sisters and brothers."[4] I felt Dr. King's determination gave courage to the people who were trying to take a stand. When he talked about his dream, he spoke of something positive, rather than condemning the situation.

His speech was a voice for change. He saw change coming. When he said, "Let freedom ring," Dr. King gave the nation a unified voice.

The movement in Selma was off the ground and receiving national attention. Additional staff members from SNCC were coming to assist—Alvery Williams, Worth Long, Silas Norman Jr., and Tom Brown. In addition, Jim Bevel, who was the director of direct action for SCLC, left Mississippi and came to Selma occasionally to keep action moving. More black citizens were attempting to register. And most important, black leaders in the community were coalescing and gaining courage to forge ahead with strategies they had learned to continue the voter registration plan. I felt this was the time that I should return to college.

I had been in and out of American Baptist and Fisk, dropping out after three years to get involved in the Freedom Rides in 1961 and returning in the spring of 1962 for a semester. When I left school again, this is when my father said, "I guess that's the end of the LaFayettes," fearing for my life in such a dangerous place as Selma. At this time I had four younger sisters, Joyce, Rozelia, Brenda, and Geraldine. My father had for years thought that I would be the only male to carry on the family name. However, he was wrong. My father had another son, Michael Anthony LaFayette, whom we lovingly called "One in a million" after a television show in the 1960s called *The Millionaire* where a man named Michael Anthony would give a check for a million dollars to random households. My father later also had another daughter, Victoria Wanda. Colia and I eventually had two sons, so that was by no means the end of the LaFayettes.

When I learned in the summer of 1963 that I was going to become a father, I made the decision to complete my bachelor's degree and take an additional job that would support my family. Although I hated to leave the Selma I had come to love, and the wonderful people I had become close to, I felt that this move was something I had to do for my expanding family. Colia and I returned to Fisk University, and in Nashville our first child, James Arthur, was born; we named him after James Forman. I was pleased to return to Selma several days a month to bolster the leaders, listen to their stories, and consult with them about what to do next. I sat in on the meetings with the SNCC organizers and continued to lend my support to the Courageous Eight.

Then I was invited to Chicago to direct the Urban Affairs Program for the American Friends Service Committee, who wanted to experiment with nonviolence in northern urban communities. Jim Lawson had presented my name to the committee as someone who had the knowledge and experience needed, and they contacted me. The Quaker Friends were committed to improving human rights and fully supported the civil rights movement. They paid a full-time salary with benefits, which was necessary for my family. I was especially happy that they were supportive of my returning to Selma each month as a consultant to carry on the work I had begun there.

The Selma movement gave impetus to the Chicago movement. In Chicago I trained black youth to become leaders and organizers in the Chicago Freedom Movement, which focused on ending slums in the city. We organized tenant unions and initiated the first effective campaign against lead poisoning. I taught gang members how to be marshals and use nonviolent direct action techniques in marches. The marches we had in Chicago had some of the same characteristics as the marches in the South. Marshals had to be prepared to give structure to the march, keep people in line, and provide a wall of protection. I regularly brought Chicago activists down with me to Selma to learn about strategy. The difference between Chicago and Selma was that whereas in the South we were dealing with violence from the white community, in the North we were dealing with violence among gang members, black gangs fighting black gangs. The question was whether or not it was possible to transform the gang members so they would stop the brutality against each other. They had to be trained in nonviolence in order to respond to the violence of fighting each other, then focus their energy on fair housing and equal justice from the white community on the West Side of Chicago.

I could relate to those gang members in a personal way, since I had some experience with being in a gang as a youth. I joined the Parrish Street Gang when my family moved to Philadelphia for a brief period during my boyhood. I was only around ten or eleven, and one condition for me to join that gang was for me to become their leader. That was a quick rise to the top! They needed someone with courage. I don't know that I was courageous, but I had a lot of nerve. We were the youngest gang in the neighborhood. All of us were little but spirited. We were willing to take on the older and bigger gangs, but we had to be fast and use strategies that worked in our favor. I even remember setting a few booby traps. We never laid a hand on the rival gang members because we wouldn't have had a prayer competing with larger and stronger teenagers. Instead we set up situations where they beat themselves. One day we collected discarded wine bottles found scattered around a vacant lot in the middle of a row of houses. We dug a trench, broke the bottles, and stuck the necks in the dirt leaving the broken ends sticking up. We covered the bottles with a layer of newspaper as a disguise, and then sprinkled sand over the papers to hold them down. Our small band of boys found the opposing gang and antagonized them by yelling until they chased us. We led them through the neighborhood and routed them straight across the vacant lot with all of us leaping over the trench. We knew they had fallen into our trap when we heard them shouting obscenities.

One night my gang got swarmed by another gang. We ran full speed into a parking lot, scattered, and each lay underneath a car, flat and silent so they wouldn't see or hear us. The old clunker I was under was leaking oil onto my head, which dripped into my eyes and trickled into my mouth, but I didn't make a sound. We stayed under those cars all night long, fearful that the other gang members were still around. At daybreak we all crawled out and ran home as fast as we could before we were missed. My bedroom was on the second floor. I shimmied up the drainpipe and sneaked back through my bedroom window. I wiped the oil out of my hair and eyes and spit the residue out of my mouth as best I could, then slid into bed, not long before it was time to get up.

It was at this young age when I first learned that there was strength and power in numbers. I learned to organize and use strategic plans that brought people together for a common cause. In Philadelphia Rev. Leon Sullivan was a name we all knew. He was a renowned Baptist preacher, civil rights leader, and social activist, whose focus was on jobs for black Americans. He requested that the large companies in the city interview blacks for positions. Only two companies responded. He initiated boycotts of businesses that didn't have equal hiring practices for blacks, using the slogan "Don't buy where you don't work." Tastykake was one of the companies that refused to comply, and this is where my gang got involved, doing what we could to support Rev. Sullivan's cause in our own small way. There were no sweets that I loved more than Tastykakes—pies, cakes, and bread. But in spite of my sweet tooth, I suggested that we all boycott not only those desserts but also the stores that sold them. It was a sacrifice for the good of a larger cause. Our gang members took turns watching for people who bought the Tastykake snacks and arranged for a little grocery "spill" as they left the store. One person refusing to purchase the foods or to stop shopping at particular stores had little effect, but when growing numbers of people joined in the boycott, it hit the stores financially and helped to bring about more desired results. Before I was a teenager I was already getting a taste of direct action and how strategies can be effective. These were the days before I had learned that nonviolence was an even more powerful force for change. When I eventually learned about nonviolent direct action, it became my most powerful realization for how to move in a positive direction. My experiences in Philadelphia showed me how gang members followed strict adherence to the orders given by a gang leader. We looked out for each other and had a commitment and loyalty to the gang as an organization, and we were willing to take risks for each other. Like the military, we didn't leave anybody behind. With good leadership, even gangs can become involved in a movement larger than themselves. When there is a common bond, it's easier to be successful since a cohesive group can make a difference. This is what happened with our little gang in Philadelphia. And this prepared me for the bigger civil rights movement. My early experiences helped me to better understand the mind-set of gang leaders and members, and more specifically, it carried over to my work with the gangs in Chicago, helping them to become involved in social action without the violence.

The longer I worked in Chicago the more I saw the same characteristics of the segregation system that were present in Selma. The Chicago realtors behaved in a similar way as the Selma registrars, regularly denying people their rights to equal housing on the basis of race. I often heard, "Things are different up north." Yes, there were different tactics, but I saw the same motives and the same results. Voting in Chicago was not an issue for blacks like it was in Selma. Yet the goal was still to keep blacks down economically and psychologically so they felt no sense of worth. When people are discouraged about inadequate incomes, insufficient resources, unequal housing opportunities, and lack of medical care, they can become convinced that they will never have those basic needs met. Then they don't perceive that they can make a difference, and they don't vote, even though they could. There was a pervasive feeling of hopelessness. Blacks weren't kept from voting in Chicago, but they didn't choose to vote because they felt their conditions wouldn't change. They didn't vote in the South because of intimidation, insulting treatment, and many roadblocks. Same result.

Two and a half weeks after the March on Washington, on September 15, 1963, one of the most tragic events of the civil rights movement occurred up the road from Selma in Birmingham. On a Sunday morning before church began, children were gathered in the basement of the Sixteenth Street Baptist Church. Dynamite exploded, blowing out an entire wall of the church and instantly killing four young black girls: Addie Mae Collins, age fourteen, Denise McNair, age eleven, Carole Robertson, age fourteen, and Cynthia Wesley, age fourteen. Twenty-two others were injured. Four Ku Klux Klansmen were arrested for the heinous crime. Dr. King delivered the eulogy for the martyred girls in that dark, sad city.

The church was targeted because it had been the perfect stage for the Birmingham campaign. It was a sizable church so it would accommodate large numbers, it was next to a public park, and it was only a short walk from downtown. I think the bombing was an attempt to threaten the movement, and like most acts of violence, it didn't try to destroy everyone. This violent act was selective and isolated, intending to intimidate and frighten people. Making examples out of a few would cause others to be more hesitant to participate. The strategy backfired. When these incidents happened, more people wanted to get involved, to support their community and to share in the suffering. In the nonviolence movement, forces continued to move forward because of the courageous leadership who wanted not to retaliate but to work even harder to bring about positive change.

Even before this church explosion, other places in Birmingham had suffered bombings. In fact the city was known as "Bombingham" because of dozens of unsolved bombings. I would have thought that if that church was going to be bombed it would have been much earlier in the movement. This was a Sunday morning; the church was filled with

Baptist churchgoers, not a mass meeting. It shook me awake to realize that there were still surprise actions to come from vicious people who wanted to stand in the way of civil rights progress.

The reaction in Selma, and my own reaction, was shock, profound sadness, and anger—and also disbelief that such a vile act would be carried out in a house of worship. It was an unsettling time, not knowing who would be next, or what city would be targeted. I was surprised that there had been no bombings in Selma. Many of us wondered why, since bombing was not uncommon in Montgomery as well as Birmingham; there had been bombings of churches, the Gaston Motel, and Dr. King's and Rev. Fred Shuttlesworth's homes, among others. Rev. Shuttlesworth was a stalwart leader of the Birmingham movement, a model and example who gave people confidence to stand up against the forces of evil every day. He was not only in the movement; the movement was in him, in his every move, whether he was walking, marching, speaking, or sleeping. He was inseparable from the struggle. Without question Rev. Shuttlesworth was a formidable force against segregation, cofounding SCLC and later serving as its national president. Although he was small in stature, his presence loomed large. His persona was the epitome of resistance.

Selma was not far from Montgomery and Birmingham, there was certainly dynamite available, and the white majority had attitudes of resistance. Yet Selma somehow escaped being bombed. I believe it was because Selma was a small town compared to Montgomery and Birmingham, and almost everybody knew each other. It was a close-knit community, not spread out and distant. Black and white neighborhoods joined each other. Brown Chapel was in the middle of a federal housing project, and had it been bombed, the federal government would have been involved. An explosion could have damaged the nearby white communities, too. Instead, white adversaries could more easily cause implosions within individuals and families. The internal conflicts could be every bit as devastating as physical attacks. The people who oppressed the blacks were individuals they saw and talked to every day, not anonymous persons. Through the system, blacks could suffer reprisal. Loans could be called in, insurance could be cancelled, jobs could be lost. Teachers in the school system were employed by the local school board and could be further oppressed by being passed over for pay raises year after year. Other tensions could be caused by firing relatives of blacks who were activists as a way of creating difficulties in their families. They didn't need to bomb Selma; they set off internal bombs in a similarly hurtful way.

Because the voter registration action had lulled over the summer months, SNCC and the Dallas County Voters League planned a way to increase motivation and muster more response for voter registration. They agreed that on one of the two days a month that the registration office was open, they would stage a mass march, bring in some power hitters, and call the event Freedom Day. On October 7 James Forman, John Lewis, the comedian Dick Gregory, the author James Baldwin, a slew of reporters, and hundreds of marchers all converged on the town and marched to the Dallas County Courthouse to line up and attempt to register to vote. It was a blazing hot day, but spirits were high and excitement was in the air. When SNCC workers began to bring water and sandwiches to the waiting marchers standing in the sun, Jim Clark and his deputies began to club them and arrest them, citing "interference" with the intended voters. Sheriff Clark shouted for the crowd to break up and leave, but they all stood in silence, refusing to move. By day's end more than three hundred people had been arrested and only a handful had been able to register to vote.[5]

This incident prompted Mrs. Boynton to contact Dr. King and seek his assistance in the Voter Registration Campaign, recognizing that his presence could lend the necessary media exposure and add new momentum to the action. The mass demonstration on Freedom Day served to give the Selma movement a shot in the arm and draw national and international attention. When popular entertainers and movement leaders are present, it serves to attract the media and dramatize an issue. In most cases Dr. King lent his support to movements that were already under way; rarely did he start a movement. He brought his presence when a campaign was lagging. This is an example of where he was called in to lend his support but also to give his leadership and direction to an already established movement. Dr. King was masterful in interpreting to the masses beyond the local community the meaning of the actions people were taking, and appealing for their support.

On Freedom Day a group of young women had been arrested and

shuffled around from jail to jail in other counties as the cells became over-crowded. Some teenagers, such as Bettie Fikes, were kept in jail for more than three weeks. They had chosen to stay in jail instead of having their bonds posted, and they chanted the motto "Jail, No Bail!" They were determined to do their part in overloading the system. We felt helpless as leaders because we couldn't alleviate the situation. They were sleeping in cold, dank jail cells with no blankets and without even their basic needs being met. I came down from Chicago to help in this situation. Out of desperation, I sought the aid of Rev. Claude Brown, the minister of the Reformed Presbyterian Church. People called him "Uncle Tom" because he was tight with white people, although I wouldn't allow people to make that derogatory reference around me. Negative labels show our narrow perspective and impose limitations rather than recognizing potential. I understood that he was getting financial support for a school, Camden Academy in Wilcox County, which educated black children. Even though he was not directly involved in the movement, he was doing something positive to help black students, and I valued those efforts. We had a good relationship and sat and talked for hours late at night. It was natural for me to try to make connections with people who seemed to have opposite positions, and to try to understand their way of thinking. I was curious and enjoyed listening to others' perspectives. He appreciated the fact that I took the time to visit.

I explained the problem about the young women in prison. None of us were allowed to go near the prison at night. We'd have been shot on sight, on the assumption that we were trying to make a jail break. Rev. Brown said he would help us under one condition: that he be allowed to do it alone. He had a church van. We said that the girls needed blankets. He elicited help from the YMCA. They sponsored camps and had cots and blankets, so they gave him blankets.

The next request was for sanitary napkins. Even though stores were closed, he knew a merchant who opened up his shop that night and gave him a whole case. Then he asked us for the oddest thing: "I need five half pints of liquor." I thought, "A preacher wants liquor?" I didn't question him, though. I just wanted the problem solved with the girls. We had enough contacts in town, so we called a liquor store owner and bought Rev. Brown the liquor he requested. He put us all to work. The minister showed us how to roll up the sanitary napkins in the blankets, and then we loaded them in the van. He put the liquor in the front seat and drove far out to the rural area where the young women were imprisoned.

When he arrived, the guards drew their guns and pointed the barrels straight at him. Then the guards recognized the church van, so they relaxed. Rev. Brown greeted them. "It's cold out here tonight and I was worried about you, so I brought a little something to warm you up," he said, and handed them the half pints. They were happy to get the liquor and chatted with him for a few minutes. Then he said, "You know those northern agitators, all they need to do is have a kid catch pneumonia in jail, drop dead, and blame it on us. So I brought some blankets. If those prisoners get sick, then it's not our fault." The guards thanked him and carried the blankets to the cells. When the girls opened them, they got the supplies they needed. The minister sat out there and talked with the guards while they drank their liquor.

We were right to give Rev. Brown the benefit of the doubt. I learned to avoid being negative toward someone simply because they don't do what I think they should do. You never can tell when they will accomplish a task that you can't do. Because he had a relationship with whites, he could go places where we couldn't go. Even though I was an organizer, I didn't have the power to persuade the adversaries or to protect our young women. It was crucial for us to convince someone to do a simple task that we had no control over, and he was the one to get the job done. Rev. Brown gave us a play-by-play description of what happened with the guards. Sometimes people feel that those who show love and compassion to others are being soft and weak. There is nothing soft or weak about it. It is also practical, as it was this night, because it helped achieve the goal. Nonviolence is about showing love toward others, and that love has the power to win people over. We were challenged in our thinking about how to help people find meaningful roles to participate. Everyone didn't have to do the same thing or take the same approach. But each role was important. That night Rev. Brown found his own way to help us meet our goal.

One of the darkest days in history was November 22, 1963, when the country lost its president, John F. Kennedy. Every television in Selma was turned on, and every eye was trained on the set, just like everywhere else in America. In sadness, I thought about Abraham Lincoln and how in a similar way President Kennedy had taken a stand for civil rights and his actions were making a difference. The people in Selma had been hopeful with Kennedy, and they were now filled with a profound sorrow and grief, having lost an influential supporter of the civil rights movement. Questions were asked: "What will it mean for our future to have Johnson, a southerner, as president?" "Will we lose the momentum we have gained?" "Will this event turn the clock back for the civil rights movement?" I imagined that these were some of the same questions that blacks asked themselves when President Lincoln was assassinated.

President Kennedy had been no ordinary friend. With the stroke of a pen he could bring about significant change. There was a pause in the movement, a necessary mourning period, and a time of uncertainty. No one could possibly know what would happen next. However, Dr. King's leadership helped us to get beyond the setback and restored our hopeful hearts. He spoke with President Johnson and with Attorney General Robert Kennedy, who reassured Dr. King that President Kennedy's commitment to civil rights was still alive. President Johnson said emphatically in his State of the Union address the following January: "Let us carry forward the plans and programs of John Fitzgerald Kennedy—not because of our sorrow or sympathy, but because they are right. . . . Unfortunately, many Americans live on the outskirts of hope—some because of their poverty, and some because of their color, and all too many because of both. Our task is to help replace their despair with opportunity. . . . Now the ideas and the ideals which he so nobly represented must and will be translated into effective action."[6]

This was a fearful time. Many of us felt that if the most powerful leaders in the world could not be protected, then the common person, particularly black persons, certainly had no protection at all. But in spite of the uncertainties of this time, we persevered. We considered ourselves soldiers in a nonviolent army and would continue to fight against violent acts with nonviolence. Violence was never a deterrent for us. We believed that if we sustained the movement in spite of the violence, we would succeed and bring about the changes we sought.

When President Johnson signed the Civil Rights Act of 1964, it was a landmark decision and the beginning of a new era for civil rights. It was universal in terms of public accommodations, not just for restaurants or buses. It covered many issues we had struggled so hard to achieve. One significant point that accompanied what we fought for was the amendment that prohibited discrimination in hiring for jobs. The burden of proof was now placed on the defendant; employers would have to prove that they were not discriminating against the hiring of black employees. Before this act, plaintiffs had to provide evidence that they were being discriminated against, and this was usually difficult to prove. I liked that the act not only included rights for people of color but also prohibited discrimination on the basis of gender, age, and physical disability, focusing on human rights. One noteworthy element about that piece of legislation that didn't go unnoticed was that it was a southern president who was taking the lead, one who had years of experience and power in the Senate, which had been a bottleneck for a lot of important changes. The fact that President Johnson was putting his weight behind the movement to end discrimination was a massive boost. He was not only making change in our laws; he was making a change in himself. Dr. King said, "The time is always right to do what is right."[7] And President Johnson did what was right.

It seemed like a pattern that with every major step forward, there was a small step back, and this continued to be true in response to the Civil Rights Act. The entire black community had been elevated by this act but immediately felt a door slam in our faces when we learned that Judge James A. Hare, a Dallas County circuit court judge, had issued an injunction that forbade more than three people to gather publicly, essentially halting the mass meetings. I was surprised that the resistance was still so deep rooted. It gave a more profound meaning to the "NEVER!" buttons. I realized that town officials were ready to fight to the bitter end with every weapon they could use to maintain the status quo. Freedom of assembly was one of our constitutional rights, and especially assembly to practice democracy, exercising the right to vote. I knew we had to work even harder and keep spirits up, focusing on all of the positive events that led up to this injunction.

In October 1964 we heard that Dr. King had been selected to receive the prestigious Nobel Peace Prize. We were so proud that this great man had been acknowledged by the entire world, to know that nonviolence works, that his message of love could be heard not just in America but in every country. He traveled halfway around the world to Oslo, Norway, to accept this award and generously donated the prize money of approximately $54,000 to the civil rights movement. To set down Dr. King's own words:

> I accept the Nobel Prize for Peace at a moment when 22 million Negroes of the United States of America are engaged in a creative battle to end the long night of racial injustice. I accept this award on behalf of a civil rights movement, which is moving with determination and a majestic scorn for risk and danger to establish a reign of freedom and a rule of justice. . . . This award which I receive on behalf of that movement is a profound recognition that nonviolence is the answer to the crucial political and moral question of our time—the need for man to overcome oppression and violence without resorting to violence and oppression.[8]

First, it was beyond our imagination that so much credibility would be given to our civil rights movement in this country. We had no idea that the world was paying attention other than some news reports. For Dr. King to be the recipient of the Nobel Peace Prize in the midst of a war that our country was waging gave us immeasurable hope that the example of our movement might be replicated by others who were struggling for social change in their respective nations. We appreciated Dr. King's inclusive approach in recognizing that there were many other organizations and individuals involved in providing leadership for this change. At the same time, we clearly recognized that it was because of his persona of nonviolence and his embrace of this philosophy from the earliest campaign in Montgomery that this movement reflected his deep nonviolent character in the face of extreme violence, assassinations, and bombings. This esteemed prize gave each one of us determination and inspiration to continue the struggle with nonviolence philosophy and methods. We were proud to note that Dr. King did not stop his work with the prize and that his eyes were still on the mountain view and the work yet to be accomplished.

The black people on the streets of Selma reacted to Dr. King's speech in a personal way. I think they felt that they were being honored because of the leadership he had given to them. He had gifted his time, his efforts, and his undivided attention for several months, which had lifted their small town to world acknowledgment. They also benefited from some of the prize money that he distributed to many organizations. Because it was a global prize, the civil rights movement received international recognition and applause. It was the first time that the prize had ever been given for a campaign that subscribed to nonviolent civil disobedience.

Every movement I participated in or organized I felt like I was laying the groundwork for Dr. King. So it was with the Alabama Voter Registration Campaign in Selma. I had continued to return to Selma from my new post working with the Chicago campaign, and enjoyed being back in the South, especially among friends in Selma. But even I recognized that coming to Selma a few days a months wasn't enough. Because SNCC was running short of money and unable to have a campaign leader there full time, the black leaders, specifically Mrs. Boynton and the Dallas County Voters League, stepped up their efforts to gain the aid of SCLC.

President Johnson had initially refused to talk to Dr. King about the Voting Rights Act, saying he had already signed the Civil Rights Bill, and that was all he was going to do just then. It was at that point that Dr. King targeted the Alabama Voter Registration Campaign headquartered in Selma. We recognized that every campaign Dr. King initiated immediately gained national attention. That's what Selma desperately needed at that point. The Birmingham campaign had ended, and Dr. King was ready to come to Selma to promote drastic action in order to increase black voter registration.

When Dr. King arrived there was a lot of press coverage. He spoke at a mass meeting to a packed house and talked about remobilizing and energizing the campaign. He said, "If they don't listen once more we will dramatize this whole situation and seek to arouse the conscience of the federal government by marching by the thousands on places of registration all over this state. When we talk about marching by the thousands, we always prepare ourselves for the follow up. If it is necessary, we are willing and must be willing to go to jail in Alabama to get the right to vote." Although the SNCC workers and I had been working in Selma for the past couple of years, Dr. King's combined efforts made a dramatic statement and breathed new life into the Alabama Voter Registration Campaign.[9]

On January 22, 1965, Charles Bonner, Cleophus Hobbs, and Terry Shaw, student leaders at the all-black Hudson High School, organized the students to walk out of school at a certain time to participate in a protest march in town. I went to the high school to see what the response was, knowing that the students had all left. I saw Mr. Yelder, the principal, hobbling down the hall on crutches from an accident.

I often went to the high school after it had dismissed for the day and talked with students. Early on when I arrived in Selma, Mr. Yelder didn't want me on the school grounds for fear of losing his job. One time he asked me to leave the premises or he would call the police and have me arrested. I left. Later I sensed a change of attitude with him.

I was glad to be back in Selma on this day because Mr. Yelder explained that he was getting ready to lead his entire staff of teachers out to the march. He agreed that it was time for them to take a stand, since the voter registration issue affected all teachers personally. Many of his well-educated teachers had arbitrarily been denied the right to vote. He asked me, "How can we have any respect from the students if we can't support what is important to them? We want to endorse the issue and also encourage the students." The teachers had spontaneously decided to march after the students left and had also encouraged him to join them. Although the school board did not give him permission, he decided to march anyway, even on crutches. I'm sure that his job was in jeopardy, but he respected and supported his teachers. There was a picture in the newspaper the next day of Mr. Yelder on crutches leading the march.

The teachers were the largest professional group in Dallas County and should have wielded a considerable amount of power. Leader Rev. Frederick Douglas Reese, the president of the Selma City Teachers' Association, had garnered the support of more than one hundred black teachers who had agreed to sign their names to a petition and march to the courthouse together. The plan was for all of the teachers to leave school at a certain time that day and meet at Clark Elementary School in order to organize and walk to the Dallas County Courthouse en masse, double file, with the intent to register to vote. The superintendent of education tried to persuade them to go back to school, to no avail. The teachers decided that they wanted only teachers on this march so that they could make a strong statement from their union.

Rev. Reese was a church pastor and a teacher. He assumed the leadership of the Dallas County Voters League as president following Mr. Boynton's death, and he was also president of the Selma City Teachers' Association. He was a resolute leader and was instrumental in the success of the Teachers' March.

It was no coincidence that Rev. Reese's effectiveness was aided by his connection to the church, the Dallas County Voters League, and the teachers' union. When there is collaboration among organizations—religious, community nonprofits, women's, and labor—these ingredients blend together to make a successful movement. These groups acted in concert with each other, largely through the efforts of Rev. Reese, who unified them in their single purpose of promoting voter registration for black citizens of Selma.

The marchers began their walk in silence. Uncertain what lay ahead, they continued with the strength that came from knowing they were all together and marching for a cause that would help not only each one of them individually but also all of their students, the future generation. In the past teachers had avoided becoming involved in civil rights issues for fear of losing their jobs from the white school board. This march was all the more powerful because it was surprising and unusual for this elite group to take such a strong and aggressive stand. I walked along on the sidewalk, beside them but not with them, as they had asked. I was proud of this group as I watched on the sidelines.

Sheriff Jim Clark had long held the notion that blacks weren't smart enough to pass the literacy tests required to register to vote. The fact that this large group of teachers was there, attempting to register, would dispel any question of inferior intelligence. I'm sure that it was a frightening experience for Jim Clark to go up against this substantial group of well-respected individuals. But true to form, he held his ground.

When the group arrived, Rev. Reese and others began their ascent up the steps of the courthouse. There, standing in wait, was Sheriff Clark, blocking the door along with his deputies. Clark wore his usual uniform with his military-looking hat tilted slightly to one side, eyes glaring down from his round, pudgy face. Rev. Reese stated in his strong, resounding voice, "We have a right to be here, to register to vote," and he asked them to step aside.

Not about to take orders from Rev. Reese, Sheriff Clark responded that the teachers were making a mockery of the courthouse and had one minute to turn around and leave. It was a long sixty seconds as everyone stood there, silent. At the end of one minute, the sheriff grabbed his billy club and shoved the marchers down the steps. He knocked some teachers down, jabbed others in the stomach, and pushed them back. But they picked themselves up and began climbing up the steps a second time. Again, the sheriff and his deputies cruelly pressed the crowd back with their clubs and bats. A third time, Rev. Reese boldly attempted to climb the steps followed by the multitude of marchers. A third time Sheriff Clark brutally thrust his billy club into their chests, knocking them back. He said, "If you don't leave I'm going to arrest all of you," to which Rev. Reese replied, "That's exactly what we want you to do." At that point someone pulled the sheriff aside and whispered something. I don't know for sure, but my guess is that he was instructed not to arrest the teachers because it would create such bad press and make him look even worse than he already did. He was so hot tempered that it was difficult for him to refrain from arresting the whole lot of teachers, but grudgingly he did resist. At that point the teachers turned around, left the courthouse, and walked to Brown Chapel, where there was a crowd of well-wishers waiting and cheering. Rev. Reese felt that this had been a successful march, a valiant attempt, and a triumphant stand.

One of the most positive outcomes of the Teachers' March was that it created a bond between teachers and students. Before this event, students had been threatened with suspension if they got involved in the movement. It was past that point now. Students, faculty, and administration were moving together for a common cause, a life cause, and a cause that affected every one of them. Another outcome was that other organizations were energized and motivated by this esteemed group of teachers to stand up for their beliefs, and the voting campaign gained a new momentum. I felt that this was one more step that moved us toward our goal of voting rights.

Sheriff Clark continued to use wholesale arrests to try to halt the movement. A SNCC worker named Lafayette Surney came to Selma to participate in a demonstration. Deputies found out that a man named Lafayette was arrested with a group of marchers and took the opportunity to rough him up. They were glad to report to Sheriff Clark that they had "beat up Lafayette in jail." Jim Clark charged into the jail expecting to see me.

When he saw Surney, Sheriff Clark said, annoyed, "What's going on here? This isn't Bernard LaFayette."

The deputy said, "His paperwork said he was Lafayette."

"Lafayette is this guy's FIRST name! This isn't Bernard!" Sheriff Clark spouted.

I saw Surney later after he was released, and he told me, "I took a beating for you."

Although I felt bad for him, I replied, "When you take the credit for my name, you also have to take the blame." I had learned that Lafayette Surney had solicited a lot of money in New York to support the movement based on my name, because many people thought "Lafayette" was me. We both had a laugh over that mistake.

On the morning of February 1, 1965, several hundred marchers gathered to go with Dr. King to the courthouse. Dr. King had mobilized the black citizens of Selma during two rousing mass meetings the night before. Although I wasn't in Selma at this time, I was told that the throng of young people who were meeting at a nearby church were prepared to follow the adult march, adding their support. As they marched along together, the sound of freedom songs rang through the streets. The public safety director, Wilson Baker, stopped the march and arrested Dr. King, Ralph Abernathy, his right-hand man, and more than 250 marchers, as planned. We couldn't get a parade permit to march because we would be in violation of Circuit Judge Hare's injunction in July 1964, forbidding groups of more than three individuals to assemble. It was Judge Hare's intention to put a halt to the mass meetings and marches, which had always mobilized support for the Voter Registration Campaign.

Among the law enforcement officials there were a few reasonable people. Wilson Baker was one such man. He was in disagreement with

Sheriff Clark over how to deal with the problems of marches and maintained a much better relationship with blacks in the community. Considered a moderate, but one who followed the letter of the law, he believed that it wasn't a violation of any law to walk into a public building, and he didn't try to block anyone from registering to vote. My only interactions with Mr. Baker were when we had demonstrations. He wasn't particularly happy when we were marching because he had to use his officers in a different way and there was always a problem with local whites trying to attack us. It put him in an uncomfortable position of having to protect the blacks from the whites who were acting up. He once said, "You have to meet nonviolence with nonviolence." But when any one of us broke the injunction, he had no choice but to arrest the violators, as he did on this day.

This was the beginning of Dr. King's dramatic move to draw national attention to the problem of voter registration for blacks. Director Baker pulled Dr. King aside and confided that he was worried about the schoolchildren, more than five hundred of whom had just been arrested by Jim Clark, and appealed to Dr. King to advise the students to go back to school, stay there, and quit marching in the streets. Most had been released to their parents, but many were being sent to a state prison farm. Dr. King told Director Baker that he appreciated his concern but that the youth had made their own decisions and would be a part of the overall settlement.[10]

While Dr. King was in the Selma jail, he wrote another powerful letter, which was not as famous as his "Letter from the Birmingham Jail," but compelling, nevertheless. In it was a list called "Instructions from the Selma Jail to Movement Associates." Thirteen points directed us, "Do following to keep national attention focused on Selma." Point number five was for me, and stated, "Bernard LaFayette: Keep some activity alive every day this week."[11] I tried to follow his instructions by scheduling mass meetings, organizing, and making sure we had continuous marches to keep people involved and momentum moving. Blacks were filling and overflowing the jails, as Dr. King had instructed, and this strategic plan was breaking the system of local government.

The most controversial and nationally recognized speaker at the mass meetings was Malcolm X, who was speaking at the nearby Tuskegee Institute. Malcolm had requested an audience with Dr. King, who was in the

Selma jail. Dr. King had said that his and Malcolm's philosophies were so opposite that he would never invite Malcolm to come to Selma during a nonviolent demonstration. At this point Malcolm had already broken with the Nation of Islam, but he still advocated a separatist position. Having returned from Mecca, he realized that many of his fellow Muslims had blond hair and blue eyes, attributes he had previously described as belonging to "devils." Accepting people of different religions and cultures, even though they were not of recent African descent, was a major shift in his thinking. He was beginning not to judge people by the color of their skin. Although he still remained a Muslim, he now embraced the larger Islamic faith, not just the black nation. He had stopped his scathing criticism of Dr. King and was reaching out and trying to reconcile with him.[12]

In Brown Chapel several of us SNCC and SCLC workers were talking and planning with a few Tuskegee Institute students and Coretta Scott King, Dr. King's cherished wife and devoted companion. While her husband was in the Selma jail, she was right there to encourage the local leadership and offer kind words of support, often participating in the meetings. She had a bright mind and excellent leadership skills, and she presented good, practical ideas in her quiet, unassuming way. Her words held power. She had assisted her husband in the first of his movements, the Montgomery Bus Boycott. We all respected her knowledge, experience, and untiring efforts to promote the cause.

The university students were telling us about Malcolm X speaking at a rally at the Tuskegee Institute, and they said that Malcolm was on his way to Selma to ask us whether he could speak at the mass meeting that afternoon. We had no idea that he was coming and only learned of this shortly before he arrived at Brown Chapel. We hardly had time to register our surprise, because there he was, walking through the doors, tall, with red hair, gray eyes, and beard. This was the first time I had seen him in person. I thought he didn't look much like a clean-cut Muslim.

Malcolm told us that since he was already in the area he would like to speak at the mass meeting in Selma, to show his support. This was a significant move for him, since it also meant that he was identifying with America as a nation; he had never advocated voting before. He looked Mrs. King in the eye and said, "I have not come to Selma to cause difficulty for Dr. King. I only want to show support." He continued to present his case to be allowed to speak. Mrs. King thanked Malcolm for coming and making an attempt to see her husband in jail. She was gracious and let him know that she and Dr. King respected him, although they didn't always agree.

For Malcolm to come here was a break from his past, when he had condemned what we were doing and espoused the rhetoric of self-defense with "an eye for an eye and a tooth for a tooth." To support Dr. King now meant that he respected the nonviolent character of the movement, even though he did not personally embrace it.

When he left, the leaders had a riveting discussion about what to do. Malcolm was well known for his oratory that often inflamed feelings and outraged people, causing them to confront law enforcement officials, sometimes causing outbreaks of violence. In the past he had condemned Dr. King and demeaned his nonviolent approach. But when I heard Malcolm state his reasons for coming to Selma, I supported his speaking because I felt that he was sincere in his attempt to move closer to our movement and to identify with Dr. King. Mrs. King also was not opposed to his speaking. However, several of the SCLC staff members and leaders weren't sure about having someone as militant as Malcolm speak. They said, "If we allow him to talk, he might start a riot and that would set us back."

I countered, "If he could undo in one speech all of the nonviolence we have accomplished in the last two years, then we don't have a very strong movement."

One role I played in Selma was that of mediator, and I worked hard to bring about a harmonious relationship between SCLC and SNCC, since they frequently differed on approach. Because I was an original organizer of the Alabama Voter Registration Campaign, I was respected by both organizations. I listened to both sides of an issue and tried to mediate some disputes. The SNCC staff members were adamant about allowing Malcolm to speak, but some SCLC members were concerned and cautious about supporting a speaker who might create a violent uprising in an intense situation. In making this consideration to allow him to speak, we had to count the cost of the repercussions we could suffer if we rejected his offer to support Dr. King.

We weighed both sides of the issue, asking, "What if we allow him to speak?" and "What if we don't?" If we had rejected his offer, it would have put us in the posture of alienating him as a person and a national leader. This would not be consistent with our nonviolent approach to winning people over. I posited that we must not judge people by their past actions, but rather be willing to accept their changes and intentions. Finally, after much debate, we all agreed to accept Malcolm X based not on his previous stand but on where he stood at the moment.

In planning the program, we had to figure out a way to accommodate his message, since we weren't sure what he would say. We decided to bookend his speech with speakers who would represent our nonviolent approach. Rev. Fred Shuttlesworth was scheduled to speak before him, and Mrs. King was slated to follow him. She was held in the utmost esteem by every person in the church. We figured if Malcolm said anything inflammatory, she could put things back into a nonviolent perspective. All of this planning was a precaution on our part, but as it turned out, it was not necessary.

Word spread that morning that the famous Malcolm X was coming to Selma and that he was endorsing Dr. King's nonviolence movement, and it was a near frenzy as people filled the church that afternoon. He was a celebrity; they had all heard about him and were excited to see him in person. Even though they didn't follow him or his separatist teachings, they appreciated his coming to support their cause.

Malcolm strode up to the podium, a tall and imposing presence. He had reddish-black hair and his trademark black glasses that made him easily recognizable. Everyone sat in silence, mesmerized. The media stood in the front, their cameras pointed and their pencils poised, ready to capture every word. He spoke powerfully and directed his words to the white media, clearly wanting his message to be heeded by the white community as well as read by the entire nation. Malcolm leaned over the pulpit and pointed his finger at them: "You had better listen to Dr. Martin Luther King Jr. or you will have to listen to me. Dr. King wants the same thing I want—Freedom!" They were stunned, shifting nervously. He gazed out at the packed church, seeming to look every man and woman straight in the eye, and admonished them to follow Dr. King. I thought his most surprising message was when he talked about our right to vote, a right we had as citizens. I knew this was a departure from his previous stance, since he used to say the Constitution was written for white people, with no consideration for African Americans because it was written during the time of slavery. There was a time when the Black Muslims wouldn't vote because they didn't consider America as their nation. Now he was declaring that we should vote.

The middle of Malcolm's speech had the most radical content, when he compared house Negroes and field Negroes back in slave days. He said:

The house Negro always looked out for his master. When the field Negroes got too much out of line, he held them back in check. He put 'em back on the plantation. The house Negro could afford to do that because he lived better than the field Negro. He ate better, he dressed better, and he lived in a better house. He lived right up next to his master—in the attic or the basement. He ate the same food his master ate and wore his same clothes. And he could talk just like his master—good diction. And he loved his master more than his master loved himself. That's why he didn't want his master hurt. If the master got sick, he'd say, "What's the matter, boss, we sick?" When the master's house caught afire, he'd try and put the fire out. He didn't want his master's house burned. He never wanted his master's property threatened. And he was more defensive of it than the master was. That was the house Negro. But then you had some field Negroes, who lived in huts, had nothing to lose. They wore the worst kind of clothes. They ate the worst food. And they caught hell. They felt the sting of the lash. They hated their master. Oh, yes, they did. If the master got sick, they'd pray that the master died. If the master's house caught afire, they'd pray for a strong wind to come along. This was the difference between the two.

And today you still have house Negroes and field Negroes. I'm a field Negro. If I can't live in the house as a human being, I'm praying for a wind to come along. If the master won't treat me right and he's sick, I'll tell the doctor to go in the other direction. But if all of us are going to live as human beings, as brothers, then I'm for a society of human beings that can practice brotherhood.[13]

Malcolm ended with, "I'm not intending to try and stir you up and make you do something that you wouldn't have done anyway." The crowd cheered and laughed with him. He continued, "I pray that God will bless you in everything that you do. . . . And I pray that all the fear that has ever been in your heart will be taken out." I recall that his final words to us were foreboding: "I am a marked man with an X on my back. I will return to Harlem, a target for assassination. And I will name my assailants." We were stunned, uncertain how to react. He left town immediately and was in Selma only about three hours, rushing to Montgomery to catch a plane back to Harlem.[14]

I was relieved that there had been little need for all the worry about his speech, as it was mostly positive and supportive of our mission. During the middle section I felt some tension, as we didn't know where he was going with his talk about the house Negro and field Negro. But all I heard in the streets the next day was buzz and excitement about this speech. People were in awe, enamored by his presence, especially to hear him support Dr. King. They were inspired that someone of his stature showed concern about their conditions. After his speech, people came to admire Malcolm X and more fully appreciate him, especially now with his more moderate position. They had already recognized his courageous stand against racism and oppression. They had heard him on the radio or seen him on TV, but now they heard him in person and listened to the articulate expression of his thoughts. Malcolm X gave them a new sense of hope because he was there to motivate them to be involved in the movement led by Dr. King.

I felt that Malcolm X and Dr. King shared some common qualities, even though they differed philosophically. One mutual point was their love of people and their determination to work hard to help people. The difference was that Dr. King embraced all people, whereas Malcolm embraced persons of African descent and those of the Muslim faith. However, after Malcolm's trip to Mecca, his vision had broadened, and he had begun to talk about the brotherhood of all mankind. A second common characteristic was that they were both articulate and charismatic speakers. They both held audiences spellbound with their genuine personalities and facility with words. Third, they both had made unparalleled courageous stands against racism and oppression. Fourth was their commitment to a greater cause, as they had both devoted their lives to the civil rights movement. They put the cause above their own personal safety and were willing to give their lives for it.

True to Malcolm's words, soon after he went back to Harlem there was a mass rally on February 21, 1965. Even though everyone was searched at the door, some men in long overcoats got through. They drew rifles and shotguns out of their coats and unloaded on Malcolm as soon as he began his speech: "My brothers and sisters . . ."

If both Malcolm X and Dr. Martin Luther King Jr. had lived, I have no doubt that those two powerful leaders would have put aside their differences and become close allies in their common struggle for civil rights. They both knew they were marked men, expecting, but not fearing, their assassinations each day of their lives. There are many choices each of us makes that affect our lives. Some choices are life changing; some choices are life ending. The time when we are born and the time that we will die most people don't know. But a few people feel the impending fate of death, and they set on a course that cannot be changed. So it was with Malcolm and Martin.

6

The March from Selma to Montgomery

I learned that courage was not the absence of fear, but the triumph
over it. The brave man is not he who does not feel afraid, but he who
conquers that fear.

—Nelson Mandela

The Voter Registration Campaign in Selma started about the same time
as the movement in Marion, Perry County, Alabama. Albert Turner, the
SCLC leader, and Dorothy Cotton and James Orange, SCLC staff, were
working in Perry County and central Alabama. James was arrested for
his work on voting rights, but he was charged specifically with contributing to the delinquency of a minor because he had involved students. He
had grown up surrounded by civil rights activists and had learned early
how to be a leader. With his impressive stature of six feet three inches,
and weight of more than three hundred pounds, his firm commitment
to nonviolence often made him appear like a gentle giant. Orange, as we
called him, carried a lot of weight in the struggle and didn't mind carrying the burden for others. He was often referred to as a foot soldier,
and he popularized the greeting that the staff used each day: "Hello,
Leader." It represented his respect for people, regardless of their station
in life. He captured Dr. King's affirmation that everybody can be great if
they're willing to serve. Orange was able to relate to people on all levels,
whether they were top-paid officials or low-paid laborers, whether they
were tribal chiefs or kitchen chefs, whether they were government leaders or gang leaders.

Orange's arrest prompted a protest march. Word spread that a group
of Klansmen was going to lynch him that evening while he was in custody.
A night demonstration was planned for people to walk together to the
jail to spotlight his illegal incarceration, to provide a wall of protection
for him, and at the same time protest the interference with voter registra-

tion. At the mass meeting in the Zion United Methodist Church before the march, Rev. C. T. Vivian gave a fiery speech, as he usually did. He spoke of the stark contrast of throwing light on James's imprisonment in the dark. Under the shroud of night, the march was far more dangerous and the risks were higher. On this particular night, the streetlights were turned off by the power company during the course of the event, so the streets were even blacker. The behavior of the law enforcement would be undetected under the cover of darkness.

Twenty-six-year-old Jimmie Lee Jackson and his entire family participated in the march, as did other families. Jimmie Lee had been actively involved in voting rights since he had been denied the right to register for about four years. State troopers attempted to stop the march, flailing their billy clubs, knocking people to the ground, and Jimmie Lee's eighty-two-year-old grandfather, his sister, and his mother were attacked along with others. When Jimmie Lee came to his mother's rescue, the police assaulted him. He started to run, and they chased him into Mack's Cafe and shot him in the stomach numerous times. He died soon after at the Good Samaritan Hospital in Selma. Jimmie Lee was the first to give his life in the Selma campaign, but, sadly, he would not be the last. On that night not only was he killed, but every member of his family suffered some atrocity. This brutal murder of an innocent, unarmed man sparked a new and vital switch from a mainly local concern to a national dialogue, beginning with the famous Selma to Montgomery March.[1]

Although I was in Selma when the Marion march happened, there were numerous SCLC and SNCC workers involved there who reported information back to us immediately. I was absolutely shocked. In the many earlier marches, there had been beatings and brutalities, but never a killing. We hadn't anticipated this happening at all. That was a significant turn of events. I didn't note any observable reaction from the white population in Selma, but the black community was outraged. The leaders knew we needed to act quickly to prevent the situation from escalating out of control into violence.

Bevel and I went to visit Jimmie Lee's family a few days later. We met his mother, Mrs. Viola Jackson, his sixteen-year-old sister, Emma Jean Jackson, and his grandfather, Mr. Cager Lee, who had a huge knot on his head from a billy club whack. They were living in dismal poverty in a "shotgun shanty" perilously perched on stacks of red bricks at the edge of a stream. This house had three rooms lined up one behind the other in a straight line—den in front, bedroom in the middle, and kitchen in the back. If a shotgun were fired in the front door, the bullet would pass through all three rooms and exit through the back door. A bleak outhouse sat behind the house. We went as clergy to share the family's profound grief, overwhelming sadness, and bitter anger. They were also concerned about their very survival because they had lost a significant source of income and they didn't know what to do.

Bevel asked Mr. Lee, "What do you think we should do about the marches?"

The grandfather replied, "We must continue. We can't stop now!"

Bevel said, "Would you be willing to lead another march in Marion?"

He immediately accepted: "I don't have anything else to lose; I have lost everything." This was the feeling for many of the families hoping to make a change. They were willing to risk losing their jobs and even their lives to support the march.

After Jimmie Lee was killed, many of the farmers in Marion were talking the language of violence. Arming themselves with guns, they told us workers that they wanted no more nonviolence. "It doesn't work," they said. "We're going to do it our way."

We found this out after we left Mr. Lee's house. Although we were planning another march in Marion, we canceled it. We were concerned that if there was another one, it would not be peaceful; that guns would be present and there would be no way to control the angry crowd. In the face of large-scale violent aggression, we had to have a large-scale nonviolent response.

The idea of a Selma to Montgomery March began with Jim Bevel. He viewed himself as one of King's apostles, perhaps even a prophet. Dr. King described Bevel as a genius, a convincing and persuasive orator, and he often followed Bevel's recommendations and advice. Bevel was a key leader in making certain decisions, and the historic march was one.

It was an important message to those who wanted to retaliate with violence that nonviolence still had power. We needed to show that Jimmie Lee's killing did not stop the movement or discourage people from participation. In fact, it had the reverse effect. Hundreds more people became actively involved. We used death as a way to shake people into life, to free those who were paralyzed by fear to understand the value of life. If we are going to make contributions in life we must do it in spite of fear; we must leap over the emotional hurdles. Fear doesn't disappear, rather it makes us jump higher over the barriers that we once thought we couldn't vault.

Instead of having another march in Marion, we decided to stage a larger event that would have impressive national impact. Bevel wanted to expand the march and made a dramatic statement to me: "I am going to walk all the way from Selma to Montgomery. I have to tell Governor George Wallace what I think about the state troopers who shot Jimmie Lee Jackson. I need to walk so I can clear my mind and plan carefully the strong message I want to deliver to Wallace. I don't want to rush, so I will walk. Do you think I could get some people to walk with me?"

I told him, "I'll walk with you. I'll walk with you for protection and for companionship."

He announced at the mass meeting that night that he was going to walk. Then he asked, "How many people are willing to walk with me?" The entire church stood up. He looked over at me and smiled, "I guess we've got ourselves a march."

We wouldn't carry the body of Jimmie Lee, but we would carry the weight of the movement and the grief of his family, and all would be empowered. The long march would give people a chance to think about the issues, to join in, and to prolong the pilgrimage. We planned for the march from Selma to Montgomery to begin in about two weeks following Jimmie Lee's death. We thought that people could walk ten miles a day, so it would take five days, which I considered perfect to prolong the pilgrimage. This direct action was designed to mobilize the nation and to have a major impact in highlighting the issue of voting rights. We knew that many people in Selma could walk only for a couple of days, so it was necessary to feed the march from the outside and increase the numbers for more impact. We appealed to people to come from all parts of the country. It no longer was a local protest, but became a national movement. Several leaders were sent to cities all over the country to bring marchers down to Selma. I returned to Chicago to attend some meetings necessary for my job, but also to recruit people from that community to come south to support the Selma march. I planned to join them on the second day.

When the first march was planned, Dr. King couldn't be there on Sunday, the first day, but it was decided that the march should begin anyway and he would join it later. Dr. King and his father copastored the Ebenezer Baptist Church in Atlanta. They alternated preaching on the first Sunday of the month, the special Sunday when communion is celebrated. It was Dr. King's turn, and he honored his commitment to his church. Rev. Ralph Abernathy, his movement colleague, was the pastor of West Hunter Baptist Church and also stayed in Atlanta to conduct his service. Rev. Abernathy was Dr. King's closest friend; theirs was a lifelong friendship that began when they were both Baptist ministers in Montgomery during the 1955 bus boycott and cofounders of SCLC. He and Dr. King spent so much of their lives together, from planning campaigns, to being cellmates in jail, to being roommates in hotels, and their lives were so intertwined, that they were sometimes referred to as the "movement twins." In private conversations Rev. Abernathy told me that he always thought their lives would end together. But fortunately, they didn't.

We expected that the marchers would trek all day down Highway 80 from Selma toward Montgomery. We had no idea how many people would show up, but we expected that it would be mostly local residents. It was left up to the individuals to make their own plans for food, water, and sleeping. Many wore their backpacks filled with food, and some carried sleeping bags, ready to spend several days and nights on the road. Some marchers made arrangements to be picked up along the way and taken back to Selma, and then resume the next day. People were scheduled to drive along behind and bring supplies. Leaders planned to return to Selma each night so they could continue planning and get a good night's sleep to be fresh to lead.

Hosea Williams was one of the highway coordinators, planning rest stops along the way, getting food to people who needed it, and assisting with restroom facilities. He was an active leader in SCLC and one of Dr. King's inner circle. After facing a number of near-death experiences, including automobile wrecks, severe beatings at which he was left for dead, and a near lynching, he was ready for anything. Early on Andrew Young joined SCLC and worked closely with several civil rights campaigns. Andy found a natural friendship with Dr. King as they both believed so fervently in nonviolent strategies for social change and were both influenced by the teachings of Gandhi. Considered a level-headed diplomat, he was always a champion for the disenfranchised. My job was to be bringing up the rear, helping everyone stay together. Church groups and labor unions worked cooperatively to coordinate the food, and they met us along the way to serve the much-needed and -appreciated meals.

Andy, Hosea, and Bevel flipped a coin to determine who would represent SCLC as leader of the march. Hosea won the toss. Later, Andrew kidded that Hosea had lost the coin toss to have to lead the march, suggesting that leading was no winning position.[2]

The leaders had prepared the crowd that they might encounter resistance. They were told to bring wet handkerchiefs in case they were teargassed so they could cover their eyes and noses. They were trained to use nonviolence no matter what happened to them.

On the day of the march there was an eerie silence, a nervousness in the air as everyone sensed something horrible was about to happen. Yet more than six hundred marchers continued on their mission, leaving Brown Chapel two by two and walking down Sylvan Street, Water Street, and Broad Street turning east to cross the Edmund Pettus Bridge. John Lewis, the chairman of SNCC, marched as an individual, since SNCC had not yet agreed to support the protest. John had been arrested many times in his activist career and always led from the front of the line, fearless and determined. We had been roommates and best friends in college in Nashville and colleagues in the struggle for many years. He was one of the leaders of the Nashville sit-in movement, one of the thirteen original Freedom Riders, and a valued associate of Dr. King's for many years. John was considered the most unlikely to survive the movement because when there was a call for a protest, he was first on the line, his chin slightly elevated, ready to walk. It was his ever-present foot on the road that put SNCC on the map.[3]

Other leaders at the front included Rev. Frederick Reese; Mrs. Boynton; Charles Mauldin, a student leader of the Selma movement; and Benny Tucker and James Austin, two of my first recruits in Selma. At the top of the bridge, marchers could see the swarm of blue uniforms of the state troopers. It looked like a posse had appeared with a herd of horses and riders armed with clubs and whips. Although a wave of fear swept across the marchers who could see this daunting spectacle, they steeled their will. Hosea and John displayed defiant resistance as they continued walking across the bridge. Both were deeply admired by their fellow leaders, as they had the capacity to overcome their fears with nerves of brass.

Captain McCloud of the Alabama State Troopers lifted his bullhorn and ordered, "It will be detrimental to your safety to continue this march. I'll say it again, this is an unlawful assembly. You are to disperse, you are ordered to disperse."[4]

Hosea Williams and John Lewis were the two most unlikely persons to obey such a command. This confrontation was not their first, nor would it be their last. They shared a common spirit of being nonviolent battering rams and threw the weight of their souls against this violent confrontation. Hosea and John knelt down, and the hundreds of marchers likewise knelt in a wave behind them. John began to pray out loud. The troopers lined up across the street and put on gas masks. They held their billy clubs out horizontally and began pushing through the crowd, knocking marchers over. Tear gas canisters were tossed into the masses, and all hell broke loose.

A sound like thunder filled the air as the horses galloped into the crowd, trampling people, whips slashing heads. Hundreds of marchers scattered, unable to breathe, eyes stinging, running toward the water to escape the gas and beatings. Others staggered back toward Brown Chapel with open wounds and blood-drenched clothes, chased by troopers on horses thrashing whips and wielding batons. Confused and injured, marchers tried to help each other while fleeing the onslaught of violence. The leaders, Hosea and John, and hundreds of others suffered bloody beatings. At the end of the day seventeen were hospitalized, including Mrs. Boynton and Mrs. Moore.

Yet from blocks away, through the breeze, the sweet sounds of voices could be heard singing "We Shall Overcome." An objective analysis would conclude that the protesters were defeated. However, from the songs in their souls, one could hear victory.

And victory it was, as this march, referred to as Bloody Sunday because of the bloodshed, increased the awareness of the important issue. Part of our strategy was to make the nation aware of the conditions people were suffering when they protested about their right to vote. As part of our plan we had informed the media. When the national audience saw the horrors, the national conscience was awakened. The public realized that violence was being heaped on people who were exercising their First Amendment rights and the government was not acting to protect the rights of citizens. Before they saw it on television it was hard to imagine, unbelievable really. Newspapers recorded in pictures and in words the terror of that experience, garnering the support of the entire nation and the world. This was the bloodiest encounter of the entire civil rights movement, and I believe that it was a defining moment in the Selma campaign.

Because I was still in Chicago when Bloody Sunday occurred, I felt helpless at a distance. When I heard the news I was stricken with grief, concerned that so many people in my beloved Selma community were hurt, possibly killed. I saw on the television screen my colleagues John Lewis and Hosea Williams, and Mrs. Boynton, the woman who had stood fearlessly against the system, being knocked down to the pavement and beaten. I stared in disbelief, feeling pain for them. And anger. I stayed glued to the television and the telephone, continuing to piece together specific information.

My response shifted quickly to that of a strategist—how could we mobilize people across the country to have an even greater march, and what would it take to get thousands of people to Selma? I immediately began to round up willing participants who were already involved in the Chicago Project, including gang members who had been trained in nonviolence, and made plans to transport them to Selma. I arranged for many cars and vans to load up with people and head down to Selma, an entire range from gang members to church members. Although I had been moving many supporters down to Selma over the past few months, I increased my efforts in order to ensure massive participation for the Selma march. They went because they viewed this as an important event that represented their beliefs and mission in life. It was an opportunity they didn't want to miss. Many stayed down there to help out in any way they could. Community members generously housed them during their Selma stay.

Fearing another outbreak of violence, Frank Johnson, a federal district court judge, issued an injunction, a restraining order that prohibited us from marching at all. In ten days there would be a hearing, so we had to wait that period. Since hundreds of people had come to join in, we felt we couldn't just sit around waiting for ten days to mobilize into action. Working within the confines of the law, we set up symbolic wooden sawhorses in front of Brown Chapel, and people stood behind the horses around the clock in shifts for ten days to illustrate the barrier to our marching. The legal barrier was the injunction. On the bridge, the physical barrier had been the policemen and horses. We wanted to keep the image of the confrontation in the minds of the nation. Dr. King used to say that when an issue is kept alive through headline news for at least ten days, then you have a movement, not just a protest march. This was a movement.

Conflict still existed between SNCC and SCLC, mostly about visibility, publicity, and money. I was asked again to be the mediator between the two organizations, and I came down from Chicago since I was needed in Selma. I tried to interpret for both groups why each organization held their particular position. SNCC had done all of the groundwork on the Voting Rights Campaign and had labored hard for two years to get to this point. Some members of SNCC felt that SCLC was usurping their campaign when Dr. King came in to lead the second march. He had just returned from talking with President Johnson about supporting a civil rights bill, which would actually be fulfilling a commitment that President Kennedy had made. Even though I was a member of SNCC, I recognized that, without question, Dr. King and SCLC were tremendous assets to winning mass appeal. When they became involved, publicity increased dramatically and gave the movement greater visibility, which led to more financial support. SNCC was simply not a strong enough presence to make the same impact. With the Nobel Prize, Dr. King was an international presence, respected and supported by a global community. He always welcomed other leaders to join him and walk beside him, not behind him. With my role as peacemaker, I tried to help SNCC members understand that the larger goal—garnering national support for the voting rights issues—was more important, and that we could reach that goal more quickly with Dr. King and SCLC's support.

It was also important for SCLC to be respectful of all the hard work SNCC had done and the grassroots support that SNCC had gained through the two previous years. Rather than pushing SNCC into the shadows, I encouraged SCLC leaders to include SNCC leaders in press conferences, to involve them in strategy meetings, and to openly recognize and praise the student organization. Both groups had their own strengths to offer the movement. I tried to maintain a good relationship with everyone to keep communication alive. Never vying for position of leadership, I wasn't a threat to anybody. Ultimately, that's how many people have come to know me, as a behind-the-scenes worker. I like getting movements started. However, I'm always looking for people to step forward to take my place. At the time I knew it was important to keep our eyes on the larger goal and not get caught up in petty differences. The mediation work seemed to be effective, as SNCC eventually threw its full support behind the march and the two groups put their differences aside and began to work together in harmony.

A day after Bloody Sunday, Dr. King returned to Selma, since he had not been there for the first march. He, along with the leaders of SCLC, SNCC, and the Dallas County Voters League, planned a second march while the injunction was still in place but had no intention of breaking the injunction. The injunction prohibited us from going across the city limits line, which was on the other side of the bridge, but it did not forbid us from marching to that line.

Two days following Bloody Sunday, Dr. King marched across the Edmund Pettus Bridge followed by hundreds of marchers. The city government didn't bother us. The state law enforcement was prepared with horses and billy clubs to uphold the injunction if we crossed the city line beyond the bridge. Flashing lights of police cars punctuated their presence. When Dr. King reached the city limits sign, he dropped down on his knees, and Rev. Abernathy prayed. The entire crowd knelt in prayer with him. When he finished, he rose; everyone turned around and walked back across the bridge. This second march helped to keep the issue in the media headlines and in the hearts of the people across the country. Dr. King called it a "Confrontation of Prayer." Critics later referred to it as "Turnaround Tuesday."

There were reasons why we chose not to break the injunction. First, we wanted to gain a favorable ruling from the federal court to allow us to march. We didn't want to get into a confrontation with the federal government, and we depended on them to enforce the Constitution, which gave us the right to vote without interference. The Voting Rights Bill, which was pending, would prohibit local authorities from interfering with our First Amendment rights. We wanted to keep a division between federal and state government. Since the state troopers shot Jimmie Lee Jackson, it had become a state issue. The federal government had the right to step in when citizens' rights were denied by the state. That's why we were going to march to Montgomery, because it was the capital of Alabama.

Judge Johnson was a liberal federal judge. Most of his rulings had been favorable for black people. Many white officials didn't like him and called him a communist because of his rulings. Forcing him to charge us with contempt of court wouldn't further our cause, so we had to use discretion in terms of selecting the issues in this campaign. We were dependent on the federal government to rectify the wrongs of the voter registration process, so we didn't want to alienate them. It was important for us to distinguish which issues would move us in the direction of our goals and which issues would divert us from them. It was clear to the leaders that the goal to focus on was the March to Montgomery to emphasize voters' rights. For example, even though police brutality was a crucial issue following Bloody Sunday, we didn't allow ourselves to get sidetracked and protest it. Our focus was kept on voting rights, and we were able to use that and mobilize more people to come. The injunction gave us the time to recruit more people, so it actually worked in our favor.

Some members of SNCC criticized SCLC and Dr. King for turning around in the second march. Many people who had come from other parts of the country were disappointed and disapproving, too, because they had traveled a great distance to walk all the way to Montgomery. However, had we broken the injunction and marched anyway, we would have been attacked and jailed. What would have been gained? Many didn't understand why Dr. King turned around. They didn't understand what the larger mission was. They didn't understand the negative impact it would have had if we had broken the federal injunction. Some were angry, others confused. But it was the right action, no question about it.

Following the second march, a horrible tragedy occurred. Rev. James Reeb, a white Unitarian minister and father of four, had flown down from Boston after receiving a telegram that Dr. King had sent to religious leaders across the country asking them to join the Voting Rights March. He and some other Unitarian ministers had an audience with President Johnson shortly before coming down to Selma. Rev. Reeb had appealed to the president to change the laws to protect people who were registering to vote. Although the president expressed empathy, he stated that he had already passed the Civil Rights Act in fulfillment of what President Kennedy had wanted. He thought he had done enough to support the movement. One thing was clear—the Vietnam War was now consuming the bulk of his attention.

After Rev. Reeb participated in the second march, he and a couple of other white ministers went to dinner at Eddie's Place, a black-owned restaurant. When they left the restaurant, the three were attacked and Rev. Reeb was struck on the head with a lead pipe. He died two days later at a Birmingham hospital. That incident enraged everyone and made us even more determined to make the march happen. Not surprisingly, it was all over the newspapers and television. The movement gained even more momentum as hundreds of people from other cities came to participate, showing support and solidarity. President Johnson was personally touched by Rev. Reeb's death. This brave man's murder underscored the importance of supporting the voting issue and the disenfranchised. The tragedy contributed to the increasing concern throughout the nation about the dire voting rights situation in Selma.

I believed that one reason why there were deadly attacks on whites was because the locals who were resisting change felt if it hadn't been for the white supporters coming down from the North, the blacks in the South wouldn't be actively fighting for their rights. Acts of violence perpetrated against whites were to discourage more whites from coming down. When I heard about Rev. Reeb, my immediate horrified thought was that they were killing clergymen, men of God. If they had no respect for the cloth, I was certain they would place absolutely no value on the lives of ordinary people, especially blacks. I feared this might increase the number of white participants coming in, which might exacerbate the violence. It put a spiritual and moral cast on the movement. It seemed that going down to Selma was like going to the cross, prepared to make the ultimate sacrifice.

A few days after the second march, President Johnson held a press conference and spoke a heartfelt message to the American people: "We all know how complex and how difficult it is to bring about basic social change in a democracy, but this complexity must not obscure the clear and simple moral issues. It is wrong to do violence to peaceful citizens in the streets of their town. It is wrong to deny Americans the right to vote. It is wrong to deny any person full equality because of the color of his skin." He also paid tribute to Rev. Reeb, saying, "One good man, a man of God, was killed." He reiterated his commitment to passing the Voting Rights Legislation, and on March 15 he introduced it to Congress.[5]

It was an exciting time to listen to these positive and encouraging words from the president. The federal government was firmly stating that we should have these rights. The passage of the Voting Rights Bill would be the modern-day equivalent of the Emancipation Proclamation and the beginning of a new Reconstruction period. Once again the federal government would uphold the rights of the former slaves and embrace them as citizens of the United States with the guarantee that their rights would be protected. This speech reaffirmed that our leadership in the nation embraced democracy for all citizens.

When the injunction was lifted ten days after the second march and we had federal court approval, we were prepared and ready to walk all the way to Montgomery. The third and final march was sanctioned by the federal government and scheduled to begin March 21, 1965. There had been a quick but massive preparation for the five-day march, which was orchestrated by Hosea Williams. We had to raise money and secure food, water, portable toilets, tents, and cots. Trucks and vans were scheduled to move the camp from one location to another for four straight nights. It was a colossal amount of preparation, but somehow, by the grace of God, it all worked out.

The morning of the march people began gathering early at Brown Chapel. We always began with a mass meeting and rally. When the church overflowed the crowd spilled out into the churchyard and into the street. In unison the crowd sang:

I want to go and march today,
march today,
march today

I want to go and march today, in Selma, Alabama.
We stand here with black and white,
black and white,
black and white
We stand here with black and white, in Selma, Alabama.
In your heart you know we're right,
know we're right,
know we're right.
In your heart you know it's right, in Selma, Alabama.
Step aside and let us by,
let us by,
let us by.
Step aside and let us by, in Selma, Alabama.

The line began to form and the leaders took their positions at the front: Hosea Williams, Rev. Reeves, Dr. King, Mrs. King, Ralph Bunche, Mrs. Abernathy, Ralph Abernathy, John Lewis, A. Philip Randolph, and Rosa Parks. Mr. Cager Lee, Jimmie Lee Jackson's grandfather, was there, proud and determined. I took my position near the end of the line in order to keep the back group walking along at the same pace. Together the procession moved forward, step by step toward Montgomery. Supporters of various races, cultures, and nationalities enthusiastically joined in—it had become a universal march. We were there to exercise our First Amendment right—freedom of speech through peaceful protest—and stand up for the original issue of voter registration.

The question had been whether we would be allowed to walk without blocking both lanes of traffic. We very well could have proceeded in single file. However, our strategy was to use the entire road, for a couple of reasons. We didn't want any traffic on the road, as people could drive by and throw things at us or, worse, run over us. It was already dangerous for the marchers. We didn't want the state troopers to escort us. Instead, we wanted federal troops to provide protection. Once Rev. Reeb was killed, it was obvious that the state could not protect the people. They had attacked us; they weren't interested in protecting us. We were only too aware that it was a state trooper who had shot Jimmie Lee Jackson.

A second reason for wanting the marchers to span the entire road was

economic reprisal. Highway 80 was a major thoroughfare for transporting goods by truck. Blocking the road for five days would have a mone-
tary impact. It would damage the state's image, and businesses wouldn't
want to invest in a place that had racial strife. The state was anxious to
get this event over and done with. In every one of our movements there
was always an economic factor that contributed to the situation in the first
place and an economic component in the solution.

Several hundred national guardsmen were interspersed throughout
the line to protect the marchers. My role was helping to coordinate the
event. I mainly worked the line, behind the scenes, organizing volunteers,
making sure the marshals were where they were supposed to be, and
guiding people in the front not to walk too fast. There were many volunteers, so we had to be thorough in taking care of people in every situation. Masses of people were lined up on the side of the street—some were
supporters, others were hecklers, and we had to deal with them in a nonviolent way. Most marchers were inexperienced, and for many this was
their first demonstration. We had to be on guard to make sure marchers
didn't respond in a way that would cause a negative reaction. Police officers and the National Guard were running up and down the line, escort-
ing us. We didn't want to give them reason to take people out of the line
or to harass them.

The mood of the march was the height of enthusiasm. People felt
good about themselves, felt good looking at their own faces in the mirror and seeing that they were standing up for something important. Some
made a decision to walk off their jobs for five days, not knowing what
the consequences would be. They knew about Rosa Parks and the boycott in Montgomery, and they knew about how peaceful marchers were
beaten and put in jail in Birmingham. Now the movement had come to
their own front porches. They didn't know what the future would hold,
but they knew that change had come in their lives and they would never
be the same. Some carried signs, "Selma NAACP" and "Civil Men for
Civil Rights."

We saw individuals who were standing on the sidelines spontaneously
step forward into the line. They weren't about to let this chance pass
them by. They recognized this moment, boldly saying with their foot-
steps, "I can be a part of this history-making event." Many were not nec-

essarily committed to nonviolence. They hadn't been trained, but the tenor of the occasion was nonviolent and they followed the discipline. Many white people on the side of the road yelled and screamed at them and called them names. But this time, they were doing something courageous rather than being casual bystanders. They were now part of the resistance. There was singing and uplifting of our spirits. Some people were chanting with the group, or singing quietly to themselves.

One song was "Ain't Gonna Let Nobody Turn Me Around":

Ain't gonna let nobody turn me around,
turn me around,
turn me around
Ain't gonna let nobody turn me around
I'm gonna keep on a-walkin',
Keep on a-talkin',
Marching up to freedom land.

Someone in the crowd would sing out a new verse and everyone would chime in. Other verses included "Ain't gonna let no Jim Clark turn me around," "Ain't gonna let no Governor Wallace turn me around," "Ain't gonna let no sheriff's posse turn me around," "Ain't gonna let no billy clubs turn me around," "Ain't gonna let no tear gas turn me around," and "Ain't gonna let no horses turn me around."

A white supporter who had come down from the North reported to us later that she was staying with a black woman. The black woman was standing in her yard holding a baby in her arms as the crowd passed her house. All of a sudden, she was so moved to join that she handed over her baby to the white woman and ran out into the street to walk with us. The white woman shouted, "Wait, what do I feed him?" In some cases the whole family joined in the protest. It was like a storm rolling in. Many were swept away in the winds of change.

Jim Letherer was a war veteran who had lost his leg in combat. But that didn't stop him. He was determined to complete the entire journey from Selma to Montgomery on crutches. He always wanted to be in the front and was concerned each day that we might leave him behind. I teased him that he wouldn't wear out a pair of shoes, but instead would wear out a pair of crutches. No matter what someone's ability or disability was, everyone wanted to be a part of this historic event.

The leaders marched by day and returned to Selma at night for meetings and planning. We received our information from all over town. There was a cook at the city jail who often overheard conversations among the officers and shared that information with us. On the second day, she knocked on the side window and warned, "Tell Rev. Bevel not to drive the car tomorrow," and disappeared into the night.

The next morning Jim stubbornly decided to ignore her words and climbed into his Nash car: "Nobody is going to tell me not to drive. I'll drive if I want to."

I said, "Let me drive. She didn't tell *me* not to drive. We don't know what's coming down so let's use the information wisely." I didn't win the argument. Sure enough, on the way to the march, the police pulled him over and showed him a warrant. There was a warrant for his arrest in Mississippi, and law enforcements had collaborated between states. He was arrested, sat in jail, and missed two days of the march.

During this period I had been traveling back and forth between Selma and Chicago, while training gang members from Chicago in nonviolence. This march became an excellent opportunity for some of the leaders to gain experience in a direct action campaign in the South. I had been training them to be marshals for the Chicago movement, and that role was ready made for Selma also. Marshals had to have courage to offer a wall of protection for the marchers. They had to be organized and disciplined and have a commitment to social change. The training had consisted of teaching nonviolent philosophy and direct action. The gang members came to understand the power of this approach by learning about Dr. King and several movements in Alabama.

Although it may seem like an impossible task to convert gang members to nonviolence, it really wasn't as difficult as it first seemed. As trainers, we tried to find out their goals and interests, then match our philosophy with what they wanted to achieve. They wanted to be marshals in a peace march. We noticed right away a number of similarities between the gang members and our typical trainees, particularly in three specific areas: courage, suffering, and loyalty. First, courage was essential. Gang members had to be courageous to protect their territory, their

community, and each other. In the civil rights movement it took courage to speak out for what was right and just. Second, they were used
to suffering for their gangs. During gang confrontations, they seldom
came out unscathed. They were willing to be the tough guys and take the
blows to protect their turf. Many even relished that role. Accepting suffering was also a factor for peace marchers, as many were injured, beaten,
and thrown in jail because they were standing up for what they believed.
Third, they were loyal to their gangs and their leaders and followed their
directives. When the gang leaders said they were going to be marshals in
Selma, the members supported the leadership, ready to do whatever it
took to make that happen. We also looked up to our leaders for guidance,
particularly Dr. King.

One notable leader, Lamar McCoy, was in the Vice Lords gang from
the West Side of Chicago. Lamar always wore a black beret, and he is fea-
tured in many photographs carrying the American flag near the front of
the march. As we trained gang members to be marshals they were given
specific roles. Since they already had courage and had scars from years
of street battles, they agreed that they would bat down the bottles that
might be thrown at the marchers. They were the buffer zone of human
flesh. They were ready to put their bodies between the bricks and the
people, if necessary. They had sworn not to resort to violence under any
circumstances. We felt they were ready to be involved in Selma, and they
did in fact play a very important role. I was confident that this experience would help them to become stronger and more committed to helping other gang members in Chicago move toward nonviolent action. In
Selma they were fighting for a bigger cause than who was going to control a block. They were fighting for a cause that was greater than themselves, giving their energy and support to others. Although they were still
warriors, they now wielded different weapons.

At the beginning of the march there were six hundred to seven hundred people. But as we neared Montgomery, the number continually
increased as thousands joined in, particularly over the last two days. More
than eighteen hundred national guardsmen were there to protect us from
the state troopers and would-be attackers. Fortunately, no one was beaten
or injured along the way.

On the last night, there was a huge rally outside of Montgomery on thirty-six acres at the City of St. Jude's, a complex of buildings that included a school, a church, and a desegregated Catholic hospital. Although it was pouring with rain that night through one mighty storm, there was sunshine in our spirits. The acclaimed singer, actor, and longtime civil rights activist Harry Belafonte organized the "Stars for Freedom" rally. For years Harry had given a great deal of support in fundraising for SNCC and SCLC. He is credited with bailing Dr. King out of the Birmingham jail, and with donating thousands of dollars from his benefit concerts to help release others from jail. He used his celebrity status to appeal to a larger audience, as well as to his fellow artists, whom he challenged to use the resources they had acquired from their talents to provide financial support to fuel the movement. This generous humanitarian financed and promoted the SNCC Freedom Singers and gave them opportunities for concerts. The Freedom Singers were a group of young people involved in various movements around the country who came together and sang freedom songs, and they became well known through the civil rights movement. They produced several albums to raise money. Harry was known for backing young artists, not only in the United States but also abroad, particularly those from his ancestral Jamaica, where he had spent his childhood living with his grandmother.

When Harry heard about the march, he conceived of the idea to have a massive rally the night before the arrival in Montgomery. He invited Sammy Davis Jr., who was performing in the musical *Golden Boy* on Broadway. Although Sammy wanted to participate, his backers didn't want to give up the money that he was bringing in for each performance. Harry wrote a check to cover the loss of revenue for one night. After the producers thought about it, they returned Harry's check and closed down the play on Broadway for one night for Sammy to support the Selma to Montgomery March. Bringing the stars down to pay tribute lifted them to the high heavens and caused them to shine.

Other notable entertainers who performed or spoke included Sidney Poitier; Nina Simone; Leonard Bernstein; Mahalia Jackson; Odetta; Johnny Mathis; Lena Horne; Peter, Paul, and Mary; Joan Baez; Pete Seeger; Tony Bennett; Shelley Winters; Frankie Laine; Dick Gregory; and James Baldwin. Many of these performers had participated in the March on Washington in 1963 and continued their commitment to the civil rights cause on this March to Montgomery. We sang freedom songs, such as "O Freedom" and "A Change Is Gonna Come." The movie stars' presence galvanized popular support for the movement.

In the middle of a muddy, mucky field, a makeshift stage was constructed from wooden crates that coffins are transported in. The crates were stacked on top of each other and enclosed in a wooden frame to secure them. Because the event was planned so quickly, this was the fastest way to construct a solid foundation. Funeral homes in the area donated the wood to support the rally.

There was such a gigantic crowd, and everyone was trying to get as close as possible to the performers. During the show, people were being pressed against the stage. When I noticed the danger, I rushed to the back to get everyone to take three steps back so the front crowd wouldn't be mashed. Eventually everyone chanted in rhythm, "Pressing people on the stage—move three steps back." It was so congested that we had to clear a path with a human chain so the performers could get through to the stage. I encouraged people to hold hands and form a semicircle. I said, "Anyone in the circle, move out. Don't let anyone back in." I tested the system by trying to get back in the circle, and they wouldn't let me in. It was working! They were following orders. I stepped back with a smile on my face. Then Sammy Davis Jr. arrived flanked with two huge bodyguards. He had just flown in from New York by private plane. The guards picked him up and carried him over the mud; his feet never touched the ground. The crowd parted with the chain of held hands, and he moved right through directly to the stage.

This memorable evening further encouraged and motivated every single marcher, as we prepared for the final day of our journey to Montgomery. With all the movie stars and singers it gave us all a feeling of genuine importance. We were honored by the presence of these famous entertainers who had come to support us. This was another way of winning over the majority of people, because all of these stars had thousands of fans. When these famous people identified with this cause, it created not just a group of stars but a constellation. The universe was certainly on the side of justice. Thanks to Harry Belafonte, a true friend to the civil rights movement.

The clouds parted; we woke up to sunshine. The rain had gone, the storm was over. On the fifth and final day, following the grand festivities, we prepared to march the final leg from St. Jude's to the capitol with great anticipation. Thousands of demonstrators had arrived the night before to join us as we ended the long journey in Montgomery, an estimated twenty-five thousand people strong. It was a beautiful day and an even more beautiful celebration of a highly successful march. We were elated that it ended without incident as people from all over the country flew, drove, and walked to the Alabama capital. Many national leaders, entertainers, movie stars, and politicians all joined in together. I stood there amazed that we were here, led by Dr. Martin Luther King Jr. on the steps of the capitol, in the middle of the Bible Belt, the Cradle of the Confederacy. Dr. King looked down the street, and in his sight was the first church that he pastored, the Dexter Avenue Baptist Church, in the city where he led his first movement, the Montgomery Bus Boycott. And now, after a decade of arrests, attacks, and even having his home bombed right here in Montgomery, he delivered his message from the seat of government to an audience of thousands. I noticed that he put his finger in his ear, which is a traditional sign that a Baptist preacher is ready to whoop. Whooping is a form of preaching, mainly practiced by black preachers. There is an intonation in the minister's voice with a musical, rhythmic repetition that connects with the spirit and emotions of the congregation. They respond in oral affirmations and chant, leading to a crescendo and, finally, squalls. People often leap to their feet, shouting, fired up, and emotional.

However, Dr. King maintained his composure and presented his poignant and poetic message, not just to a Baptist church audience but to an entire world, as the media transmitted his words internationally. Dr. King delivered one of the most powerful speeches of his life, often referred to as the "How Long, Not Long" speech. His eloquent words filled the air and our hearts: "The end we seek is a society at peace with itself, a society that can live with its conscience. And that will be a day not of the white man, not of the black man. That will be the day of man as man."[6] He had a remarkable ability to communicate effectively not only with scholars in ivory towers but also with the common people in the pews on Sunday morning, and with each person in the street that day. He had the voice but never relied solely on his homiletic gifts. He talked as a statesman speaking to his government and its people. His messages were always inspiring, informative, and motivating. So it was on this historic occasion. At the conclusion of the march and Dr. King's speech there was a feeling that the goal of the Voting Rights Movement was within reach. We felt with all confidence in our minds, our hearts, and our feet that soon we would all be marching to the voting booths.

At the culmination on the steps of the Alabama State Capitol there was a feeling that a barrier had been broken. All the symbols of resistance from the governor's office had been overcome. It was clear that the support from around the country was unquestionably the sentiment of the majority of the American population. I believe that Dr. King was right when he had said several years previously, "The key to everything is federal commitment."[7]

When the march ended there was a mass exodus from Montgomery. The airport was packed with people flying home to cities all across the country. Those who had walked the entire fifty-four miles needed some way to return to Selma. I was at the black-owned Brown Hotel in Montgomery, where all the leaders were staying, planning to return to Selma that day. Rumors were circulating that as a repercussion to the march, people were being killed randomly in Selma, but we found out later it wasn't true.

However, someone had been killed on the highway. Sadly, this was not a rumor. Viola Liuzzo, a dedicated white activist and mother of five, had left her home and family in Detroit to come down to Alabama to help in any way she could. She used her car to shuttle people back to Selma all evening, five at a time. Viola was driving back to Montgomery to pick up another load of people. Leroy Moton, a young black teenager from Selma, was in the car with her. A carload of Ku Klux Klan members drove up beside her and shot into the car. Her car crashed and rolled into a ditch. Leroy fell into her lap and was covered with blood—Viola's blood. He raised his head and saw the white men coming toward the car. He put his head back down in her lap and remained as still as death. They looked in the car and concluded that she was dead. There was so much blood on Leroy's head that they thought he was dead, too. Slowly, Leroy lifted his head, peering through the shattered glass of the windshield to make sure they had left the scene. He dragged himself out of the car and stumbled up to the highway to get help for his driver, but it was too late.

Viola had been so moved by the story of Jimmie Lee Jackson that she had come to Selma, responding to the death of one black man. Ironically, she was shot and killed, saving another young black man with her own blood. The details of what happened were later revealed because one of the men in the other car was an FBI informant who had infiltrated the group. Often when there is a successful direct action campaign there is a reaction to it. Some reaction, although not unexpected, is always heartbreaking. There was intense grief that this celebratory day should end in tragedy.

When I first heard about Viola's death, Stokely Carmichael and I were at a church gathering in Lowndes County on Highway 80. A person from the news media came by and told us. We left immediately and headed back to Selma on the same road that Viola had been driving. It was a long and sad, sad night. We felt the need to go to Selma to help and console the people there. So many people in Selma felt anger, hurt, and profound heartbreak. Also there was fear and anxiety, not knowing whether others would also be targeted. We realized that we had no control over who might be killed and that we couldn't protect the lives of those who had already made tremendous sacrifices to be involved in the cause of civil rights. We also recognized that there was nothing any of us could have done to save her. It was a quiet town that night, a completely different atmosphere than when we had left five days earlier.

I feel that sometimes death causes us to have a greater appreciation of life. The day was bittersweet as we celebrated a victory and also commemorated a courageous woman who nobly gave her life for a worthy cause. The contributions and sacrifices of those who died will always be remembered. I still have mixed emotions when I reflect on those who gave their lives so selflessly, particularly Viola Liuzzo because I knew her and valued her as a human being and for what she had personally contributed. She drove me from the Birmingham airport to Selma along with Diane Nash Bevel's uncle, Evander Ross, who was a skycap from Chicago. There's not a time that I drive past the monument that marks the area where she was killed that I don't reflect on that tragic night and say a silent prayer for her and for the family she left behind. I always reminisce about my airport drive with her and about how she sacrificed her life so that others might live and enjoy freedom and democracy in their own nation.

There is power in a collective effort. Rather than "*I* will overcome," the march helped us all to focus on "*We* shall overcome—together." One individual may not bring about change, but a group can organize a massive effort and yield a stronger impact. This is the difference between a personal protest and a movement. Even though people are still individuals, they can play their part in the whole effort. In Selma, outsiders traveled from around the nation to support our cause. The outsiders were able to bring their support to the movement because they recognized the truth of Dr. King's statement "Injustice anywhere is a threat to justice everywhere," and they felt its effects. The movement was no longer just the small local community; it became a national movement when we won the outside support of thousands across the country.

7

Reflections on the Alabama Voter Registration Campaign

You must be the change you wish to see in the world.
—Gandhi

The most significant outcome of the Alabama Voter Registration Campaign was the passage of the Voting Rights Act of 1965, signed into law by President Lyndon B. Johnson on August 6, which banned racial discrimination and secured equal voting rights for black citizens. This resulted in a dramatic increase in voter registration for African Americans. The Voting Rights Act is considered by many people to be the single most important legislation for civil rights. It restored the right to vote guaranteed by the Fourteenth and Fifteenth Amendments to the Constitution, which stated that no individual should be denied the right to vote because of race. In addition, it eliminated the use of the unfair literacy tests, poll taxes, and other discriminatory practices to prohibit people from registering to vote. The Voting Rights Act was a direct consequence of the Alabama Voter Registration Campaign. I'm proud to say that the work that was done in Dallas County and surrounding counties began a positive change throughout the southern states. By the summer following the signing of the Voting Rights Act, more than nine thousand black voters were registered, giving them back the voice that had been oppressed.[1]

I learned from Dr. King the importance of transforming the way people think, not just changing the laws. At the end of the march we never boasted "We won!" as if we had defeated an enemy. Even when the laws change, it is necessary to win the hearts of the opposing people to be truly effective. You can smile at your adversaries but not stick out your tongue. When the Voting Rights Act of 1965 was passed, it was critical for people's thinking to have changed so that the laws could actually work. Dr.

143

King once told me that laws could regulate people's behavior but not necessarily their hearts.

When people's thinking changes, it affects how they view other issues of injustice. Once they have a change of heart, they may not accept other unjust conditions. It's not the people in the movement that's important; it's the movement in the people that counts. I'm certain that the way the Selma community thought about themselves was revolutionized. Changing a law will make a difference only if people have changed inside.

I believe that a secondary result, but nevertheless an important one, was that people saw the power of nonviolence and recognized that they had the ability to stand up for their beliefs. Their actions of protesting injustices could bring about transformation. Blacks realized that they had the capacity to change unfair and oppressive conditions. They grasped the idea that they, as ordinary individuals, had a role to play. When they combined their individual strengths with strengths of others, they multiplied many times their reservoir of resources.

Going through the experience of Selma gave me a new set of skills and enriched the skills I had already acquired. I felt ready to take on Chicago, applying the principles, steps, and philosophy that I had embraced from the early days in Nashville and the Freedom Rides, and that I had continued through Selma. I also recalled some of my narrow escapes, and friends who weren't as fortunate. That responsibility weighed heavy on me, and I vowed to make sure that those who sacrificed their lives did not give them in vain. The road that led to the Voting Rights Act of 1965 was drenched with blood: not necessarily the blood of our resisters or our opponents, but the blood of advocates and supporters. I wanted to share these experiences not simply for them to be clarified in the minds of researchers, but to be lessons for those who want to apply these nonviolent approaches to dealing with current problems in their lives and communities on national and global levels.

I'm often asked whether I ever got depressed or lost hope through the years of struggle. Honestly, I can say that I never experienced the down moments that some leaders have. Some of the aggravation for Dr. King came from a few of the people who were supposed to back him, and it wore him down. I never had that dissension around me but was always bolstered by individuals with high spirits. In Selma I never had to stand alone, with key supporters such as Mrs. Boynton, Rev. Anderson, Rev. Reese, Mrs. Foster, Mrs. Moore, Mr. Moss, Mr. Gildersleeve, and Father Ouellet. The students who surrounded me gave me so much inspiration and hope for the future. I felt a protective shield with Attorney Chestnut by my side, knowing that a belligerent sheriff or oppressive town leaders weren't going to be able to trap me in legal entanglements. These colleagues were giants who acted without fear. I never received death threats over the phone, as Dr. King did. Any setbacks we had, I didn't worry because I knew these friends would be right there standing beside me, giving me the confidence and courage to carry on, no matter what happened. I tried to view each small step as a success. Most important, my faith always sustained me through many difficult times.

From the beginning, I didn't really expect to survive the movement. I was actually surprised that I made it through two years in Selma relatively unscathed. The most down period I have ever had in my life was when Dr. King was assassinated. The question lingered in my mind why more of us weren't assassinated. I thought we might be picked off one by one. But we weren't. When Dr. King was killed it was a time of transition and rethinking, knowing everything would change. I thought long and hard about how I could serve most effectively, and I deeply felt that I needed to complete my college education. I returned to school, this time with a serious commitment, and not only received a bachelor's degree from American Baptist Theological Seminary but went on to earn a master's degree and doctorate from Harvard in a period of five years. I've tried to use my education in a way Dr. King would have wanted, to continue to train others to use nonviolent direct action as a positive force in bringing about needed change.

It was inconceivable when I was in Selma that we'd ever have a black president during my lifetime, especially the caliber of person who won the confidence of the voters as President Obama did. I don't think he was elected solely because he was black, but because he was someone who assured the American public that he could provide the most effective leadership that was needed at the time. He just happened to be black. The fact that President Obama was elected renews my confidence in our country. That it is possible for us to put race aside and choose the finest candidate based on our best judgment is exhilarating. We have to recognize that the large number of blacks who voted was no small factor in electing President Obama. Before the Voting Rights Act of 1965, I recall such small numbers of blacks in the South being able to vote because blacks were denied the opportunity. Removing the barriers inspired blacks to participate in government not only by voting in their community, state, and country but by becoming candidates for office and being elected to the Congress and Senate, and now the presidency. The Voting Rights Act didn't just favor the southern states by enfranchising the black community; it helped the entire nation.

I love to go back to Selma in March every year when the town celebrates that historic march with a jubilee. I want everyone to see the physical scene and to walk on the ground where courageous people made their statement to the world, to revisit that pivotal moment in history. My visits have more to do with helping others understand the significance of what happened there and to feel a deeper appreciation of this movement and how it succeeded, rather than just reliving it myself. It's of great consequence for the young people to meet some of the key players who made it happen, to bring those events alive that they have only read about. Mostly, I want all who visit the Selma Museum and walk across the Edmund Pettus Bridge to understand that the philosophy of nonviolence can help them cross many bridges in their own lives.

My mission was accomplished during the two years of working in Selma. I felt that the part I played in getting things started then fading back and allowing the natural leadership of the community to emerge was not only strategically correct; it was my personal design to push that leadership forward. I was proud that I was able to work effectively within the community to bring about specific changes in the voter registration process. Equally important, I was honored to have worked closely with such an amazing group of individuals who helped the people in the Black Belt of Alabama transform internally. They also realized that they had the power to effect change when they worked together toward a common goal. Although it was just one campaign, I believe that the lessons learned from Selma can generalize to other movements. It was a huge national triumph that began in one small Alabama town.

Epilogue

The Road Out of Selma, March 1965

Change does not roll in on the wheels of inevitability, but comes through continuous struggle. And so we must straighten our backs and work for our freedom.

—Dr. Martin Luther King Jr.

As I drove out of Selma in 1965, along Highway 80, I pondered what an important stretch of road this was that had led not only to Montgomery but to the passage of the Voting Rights Act of 1965. I recalled the thousands of hopeful marchers moving along this pavement step by step toward justice. I reminisced about that fall day when I first drove to Selma along this same route and the accident I had come upon. Remembering the elderly black man who was so frightened talking to the white police officers about the crash, I could only hope that over the two years that had since passed he might have gained some confidence and hope. I thought about my grandmother, Ma Foster, who inspired me at an early age to find the positive in the negative and to view the impossible as possible. She taught me to persevere in the face of difficulties and to never lose faith. With the drama and the trauma that Selma had experienced over the past two years, I knew that the community would never be the same.

In 1963 Selma was a small, quiet, rural town. By 1965 Selma had made its mark in history and was nationally recognized as a battleground in the civil rights movement that introduced one of the most important victories for social change in our nation. The people who participated in this movement, both those in Selma and those who came to Selma, displayed incomparable courage. When the Voting Rights Act was passed, not only was there cause for celebration for those directly involved, but it was also a moment of pride for the entire nation. It set a powerful example for the rest of the world.

I've traveled a long way from Selma and journeyed many miles since leaving Alabama. But the lessons I learned there have steered me throughout my lifetime of work in nonviolence, education, and activism. Training in nonviolent direct action kept the movement peaceful on the part of the protesters and helped the nation see the oppressive environment that existed in Alabama. We won the sympathy of the nation and the support of the majority. The experiences from Selma have guided me through the difficult challenges I faced in Chicago, Memphis, and the aftermath of Dr. King's assassination, the troubles of coordinating the Poor People's Campaign, and in establishing nonviolent centers in Colombia and Africa. Each day I recall Dr. King's last words to me in Memphis the morning he was killed: "Bernard, the next and most important campaign we need to focus on is institutionalizing and internationalizing nonviolence." I made this my life's mission, and for most of the past half century I have strived to live out his words. No matter what I have done or what job I have had, nonviolence has always been my vocation and the way I travel every road of my life's journey.

Afterword

Bernard LaFayette Jr.'s riveting account of his experiences in Selma reminds us that the realization of America's democratic ideals has rarely involved an easy or uncontested march to victory. During the 1960s, civil rights activists in the Deep South faced powerful adversaries determined to defend the traditions and shibboleths of racial privilege and prejudice by any and all means. Part of the problem, as this book reveals in fascinating detail, resided in personal and political chicanery, but the movement for democratization and racial justice also had to deal with institutional inertia and a pervasive popular complacency. Before meaningful change could occur in the lives of African Americans, the structural bulwarks of disfranchisement and second-class citizenship had to be confronted and identified in dramatic fashion, highlighted in a way that would disrupt and confound long-standing political and social conventions. As we have seen, this instrumental drama was exactly what Bernard LaFayette and others accomplished in Selma.

In the late winter of 1965, a full ninety-five years after the passage of the Thirteenth Amendment, the struggle to secure the voting rights guaranteed by that amendment finally commanded national attention. The epicenter of the struggle was a small Black Belt Alabama town where hundreds of nonviolent activists were beaten by state and local police, and where thousands more ultimately gathered for a protest march to the state capitol in Montgomery. By the time President Lyndon Johnson signed the Voting Rights Act into law in late July, "Bloody Sunday" and the Selma to Montgomery March had become iconic elements of the civil rights saga. All of this took much of the nation by surprise. Before the dramatic events that unfolded on the Edmund Pettus Bridge and on the road to Montgomery, few Americans had ever heard of Selma, and no one outside of the civil rights movement's inner circle knew any of the backstory that had precipitated the Selma crisis.

That backstory—the long-hidden, behind-the-scenes struggle to generate and sustain the local Selma movement—is the subject of Bernard LaFayette Jr.'s remarkable memoir. Though only twenty-two years old when he arrived in Selma in the fall of 1962, LaFayette was already a seasoned veteran of the civil rights struggle. In 1959 and 1960, at the age of nineteen, he had become deeply involved in the Nashville Student Movement, attending nonviolence workshops conducted by Rev. James Lawson and joining other student activists, including several of his classmates at the American Baptist Theological Seminary, in a series of sit-ins and protest marches. In May 1961 he became a Freedom Rider, boarding a series of buses in Alabama in a brave effort to test compliance with two U.S. Supreme Court decisions mandating the desegregation of interstate travel. Arrested in Jackson, Mississippi, he became one of more than three hundred Freedom Riders incarcerated in Parchman Prison during the spring and summer of 1961. Following his release from prison in early July, he, unlike most Freedom Riders, remained in Mississippi, where he helped James Bevel and Diane Nash to organize the Jackson Nonviolent Movement. This effort, which involved recruiting black teenagers, led to an arrest for contributing to the delinquency of minors. After being convicted and released pending an appeal, he resumed his involvement in the Mississippi civil rights struggle—editing the Jackson movement newsletter—and in the wider politics of the Student Nonviolent Coordinating Committee (SNCC).

In mid-August, he attended a memorable conference at the Highlander Folk School in Monteagle, Tennessee, where a gathering of SNCC activists reconfigured the organization into two wings: one devoted to nonviolent direct action and the other to voting rights advocacy. During three days of debate and sometimes sharp disagreements, LaFayette played the role of peacemaker, counseling his fellow activists that both direct action and voting rights were essential to SNCC's mission. "A bird needs two wings to fly," he reminded his departing colleagues.

Following the Highlander meeting, SNCC's executive secretary, James Forman, dispatched LaFayette to Detroit on a special fundraising mission. Three SNCC voting rights workers were in jail in Louisiana, and the organization needed $30,000 in bond money to arrange their release. After spending several weeks in Chicago raising the money, LaFayette eagerly returned to the South with the expectation that he would be assigned to the directorship of a major SNCC voting rights project. To his dismay, however, all of the directorships had already been parceled out. The only possible assignment was to set up an Alabama Voter Registration Campaign headquartered in Selma, but that alternative didn't seem very promising: a discouraging preliminary investigation of the local racial situation had led Forman to scratch the Alabama campaign from the list of authorized projects. Seeing LaFayette's disappointment, Forman reversed his decision, reinstating the plan for the Selma-based campaign. But he clearly held out little hope that it would amount to much.

Forman's reluctant reversal—and LaFayette's acceptance of the unpromising Selma assignment—represented one of the important turning points in the long history of the voting rights struggle. The local movement that LaFayette and SNCC nurtured—the movement that Dr. King and the Southern Christian Leadership Conference (SCLC) later enlisted in a national campaign for equal citizenship—not only brought a measure of voting rights to Selma and the surrounding communities of the Alabama Black Belt; it also exposed the violent underpinnings of white supremacist politics, cracked the mystique of Jim Crow in the Deep South, and prompted federal legislation that changed the character of American democracy. Since his years in Selma, LaFayette has enjoyed a long and distinguished career as an activist and educator, serving as a minister and theologian, a college president, the national coordinator of the 1968 Poor People's Campaign, the director of the Center for Nonviolence and Peace Studies at the University of Rhode Island, the chair of SCLC's National Board, an internationally acclaimed trainer in Kingian nonviolence, and Distinguished Senior Scholar at Emory University in Atlanta. But none of his many noteworthy accomplishments looms larger than what he wrought as a young man of faith and courage in central Alabama a half century ago. True to his character, LaFayette relates this unlikely story of democratic promise and purposeful action with an uncommon mix of humility, treasured memory, and reflective wisdom.

Raymond Arsenault
John Hope Franklin Professor of Southern History
University of South Florida, St. Petersburg

Acknowledgments

I wish to express deep appreciation for those of you who played a role in making this book a quality documentary that will contribute to the rich history of the civil rights movement and nonviolent struggle that occurred in Selma, Alabama. To the courageous people of Selma, this book was inspired by you and is for you. George Bulls II, this publication would not have happened without your consistent and tenacious efforts. Your untiring and generous labor made it possible to execute the details necessary for the timely publication. Sam Walker from the National Voting Rights Museum in Selma, I value your assistance in obtaining some essential photographs and material that enhanced this publication. Many, many thanks, Professor Paul Bueno de Mesquita, director of the University of Rhode Island's Center for Nonviolence and Peace Studies, for sage advice and astute recommendations, and for giving up time with your wife for endless hours through three years while Kay and I worked together on this memoir.

At the University Press of Kentucky, a shout to Bailey Johnson for your bighearted spirit and for always answering questions immediately. Anne Dean Watkins, what a positive force you are. You patiently waited for us to complete the manuscript and were a powerful advocate for this book—you are the best. Cynthia Fleming, we owe a great debt to you for the constant guidance and wisdom as you read several drafts and nudged us to be our best. Connie Curry, you not only were a remarkable mentor to me in the '60s but have continued to inspire me for more than fifty years. Your comments and suggestions on the manuscript were immensely helpful. Finally, an enormous thank-you to our family and friends who encouraged and supported us in infinite ways. We can never express enough the boundless appreciation that fills our hearts.

This book is dedicated to the four women who have had the most important influence on my life: three in my earlier years, and one who has influenced me for the past forty years and continues to do so.

First, my maternal grandmother, Rozelia Forrester, lovingly known as "Ma Foster," a woman who was independent, daring, courageous, wise, generous, and a firm disciplinarian. She was a businesswoman and a devout Christian home missionary who owned and operated a grocery store and small animal farm. She helped to found a church, the New Hope Missionary Baptist Church in Tampa, and built a congregation. She was my teacher and spiritual mentor, and she played a great role in my pursuit of higher education.

Second is my mother, Verdell LaFayette, who treated me special from birth. Her love and prayers brought me through when times seemed impossible. Sometimes she was like a big sister, other times an imitation of my grandmother. Since she knew me so well, she knew what strategy would get me to do what she wanted me to do. My grandmother got me into college, but it was my mother who motivated me to finish it. She used what I call negative inspiration. She'd tell me, "You will never finish college." I would reply, "Yes, I will." She'd say, "Oh, no, you won't." I was determined to prove her wrong, which was what she wanted me to do. I was in and out of college for years, but eventually I handed her a doctoral degree from Harvard University. We both won.

The third was Amelia Boynton, who inspired me to take on one of the most difficult challenges in my life: Selma, Alabama. She encouraged me and stood by me, and every day she was a glowing example of courage, quiet defiance, and determination, and a reservoir of generosity. I knew every moment I was in Selma that I was not alone, and what better mentor could one have than Mrs. Amelia Boynton? Her leadership was similar to that of Dr. Martin Luther King Jr., bringing others to the forefront and then standing with them. It was her eternal optimism and hope that made the Selma movement possible. She helped me to grow from a young college student to a man in a short period. When one has to make decisions that will determine life or death, one understands what adulthood and manhood are all about.

Finally, my loving wife, Kate Bulls LaFayette. Because of her, I was able to hand my mother my terminal higher education degree. She supported me in every way and encouraged me even when I had doubts about completing my education. She made it possible for me to support my two sons, James Arthur and Bernard III, during their early years and stages of development. Because of her background in early childhood education, she could relate to them, not only as a stepmother but as a molder of values and character. Kate has worked with me, has walked with me, and has sometimes waited patiently for me until I caught up. Without her I would not have been able to accomplish the many goals in my life and would not be able to achieve my purpose for the future. Her love, her strengths, her wit, and her wisdom have made my pilgrimage in life an exciting yet peaceful adventure. How sweet it is! Thank you, Kate. I love you.

Appendix A

Example of a Literacy Test for Registering to Vote*

Part A

[Part "A" of the Literacy Test required the applicant to read aloud from a section of the U.S. Constitution, explain it, and write a portion of it to the satisfaction of the registrar.]

Part B

1. What body can try impeachments of the president of the United States?

_____

2. Check the applicable definition for responsibility
_____ a duty
_____ a speech
_____ failure

3. Name the attorney general of the United States. _____

_____

4. Women may now serve on juries in Alabama State courts. _____
(T/F)

Part C

1. If a person charged with treason denies his guilt, how many persons must testify against him before he can be convicted? _____

2. At what time of day on January 20 each four years does the term of the president of the United States end? _____

3. If the president does not wish to sign a bill, how many days is he allowed in which to return it to Congress for reconsideration? _____

4. If a bill is passed by Congress and the President refuses to sign it and does not send it back to Congress in session within the specified period of time, is the bill defeated or does it become law? _____

_____

*Source: http://www.crmvet.org/info/lithome.htm.

Appendix B

Excerpt from President Lyndon B. Johnson's Special Message to the Congress: "The American Promise"*

The following speech was delivered in person on March 15, 1965, at 9:02 P.M. before a joint session. The address was broadcast nationally.

Mr. Speaker, Mr. Vice President, Members of the Congress:

I speak tonight for the dignity of man and the destiny of democracy. I urge every member of both parties, Americans of all religions and of all colors, from every section of this country, to join me in that cause.

At times history and fate meet at a single time in a single place to shape a turning point in man's unending search for freedom. So it was at Lexington and Concord. So it was a century ago at Appomattox. So it was last week in Selma, Alabama.

There, long-suffering men and women peacefully protested the denial of their rights as Americans. Many were brutally assaulted. One good man, a man of God, was killed.

There is no cause for pride in what has happened in Selma. There is no cause for self-satisfaction in the long denial of equal rights of millions of Americans. But there is cause for hope and for faith in our democracy in what is happening here tonight.

For the cries of pain and the hymns and protests of oppressed people have summoned into convocation all the majesty of this great Government—the Government of the greatest Nation on earth.

Our mission is at once the oldest and the most basic of this country: to right wrong, to do justice, to serve man.

In our time we have come to live with moments of great crisis. Our lives have been marked with debate about great issues; issues of war and peace, issues of prosperity and depression. But rarely in any time does an issue lay bare the secret heart of America itself. Rarely are we met with a challenge, not to our growth or abundance, our welfare or our security, but rather to the values and the purposes and the meaning of our beloved Nation.

The issue of equal rights for American Negroes is such an issue. And should we defeat every enemy, should we double our wealth and conquer the stars, and still be unequal to this issue, then we will have failed as a people and as a nation.

For with a country as with a person, "What is a man profited, if he shall gain the whole world, and lose his own soul?"

There is no Negro problem. There is no Southern problem. There is no Northern problem. There is only an American problem. And we are met here tonight as Americans—not as Democrats or Republicans—we are met here as Americans to solve that problem.

This was the first nation in the history of the world to be founded with a purpose. The great phrases of that purpose still sound in every American heart, North and South: "All men are created equal"—"government by consent of the governed"—"give me liberty or give me death." Well, those are not just clever words, or those are not just empty theories. In their name Americans have fought and died for two centuries, and tonight around the world they stand there as guardians of our liberty, risking their lives.

Those words are a promise to every citizen that he shall share in the dignity of man. This dignity cannot be found in a man's possessions; it cannot be found in his power, or in his position. It really rests on his right to be treated as a man equal in opportunity to all others. It says that he shall share in freedom, he shall choose his leaders, educate his children, and provide for his family according to his ability and his merits as a human being.

To apply any other test—to deny a man his hopes because of his color or race, his religion or the place of his birth—is not only to do injustice, it is to deny America and to dishonor the dead who gave their lives for American freedom.

The Right to Vote

Our fathers believed that if this noble view of the rights of man was to flourish, it must be rooted in democracy. The most basic right of all was the right to choose your own leaders. The history of this country, in large measure, is the history of the expansion of that right to all of our people.

Many of the issues of civil rights are very complex and most difficult. But about this there can and should be no argument. Every American citizen must have an equal right to vote. There is no reason which can excuse the denial of that right. There is no duty which weighs more heavily on us than the duty we have to ensure that right.

Yet the harsh fact is that in many places in this country men and women are kept from voting simply because they are Negroes.

Every device of which human ingenuity is capable has been used to deny this right. The Negro citizen may go to register only to be told that the day is wrong, or the hour is late, or the official in charge is absent. And if he persists, and if he manages to present himself to the registrar, he may be disqualified because he did not spell out his middle name or because he abbreviated a word on the application.

And if he manages to fill out an application he is given a test. The registrar is the sole judge of whether he passes this test. He may be asked to recite the entire Constitution, or explain the most complex provisions of State law. And even a college degree cannot be used to prove that he can read and write.

For the fact is that the only way to pass these barriers is to show a white skin.

Experience has clearly shown that the existing process of law cannot overcome systematic and ingenious discrimination. No law that we now have on the books—and I have helped to put three of them there—can ensure the right to vote when local officials are determined to deny it.

In such a case our duty must be clear to all of us. The Constitution says that no person shall be kept from voting because of his race or his color. We have all sworn an oath before God to support and to defend that Constitution. We must now act in obedience to that oath.

Guaranteeing the Right to Vote

Wednesday I will send to Congress a law designed to eliminate illegal barriers to the right to vote.

The broad principles of that bill will be in the hands of the Democratic and Republican leaders tomorrow. After they have reviewed it, it will come here formally as a bill. I am grateful for this opportunity to come here tonight at the invitation of the leadership to reason with my friends, to give them my views, and to visit with my former colleagues.

I have had prepared a more comprehensive analysis of the legislation which I had intended to transmit to the clerk tomorrow but which I will submit to the clerks tonight. But I want to really discuss with you now briefly the main proposals of this legislation.

This bill will strike down restrictions to voting in all elections—Federal, State, and local—which have been used to deny Negroes the right to vote.

This bill will establish a simple, uniform standard which cannot be used, however ingenious the effort, to flout our Constitution.

It will provide for citizens to be registered by officials of the United States Government if the State officials refuse to register them.

It will eliminate tedious, unnecessary lawsuits, which delay the right to vote.

Finally, this legislation will ensure that properly registered individuals are not prohibited from voting.

I will welcome the suggestions from all of the Members of Congress—I have no doubt that I will get some—on ways and means to strengthen this law and to make it effective. But experience has plainly shown that this is the only path to carry out the command of the Constitution.

To those who seek to avoid action by their National Government in their own communities; who want to and who seek to maintain purely local control over elections, the answer is simple:

Open your polling places to all your people.

Allow men and women to register and vote whatever the color of their skin.

Extend the rights of citizenship to every citizen of this land.

The Need for Action

There is no constitutional issue here. The command of the Constitution is plain.

There is no moral issue. It is wrong—deadly wrong—to deny any of your fellow Americans the right to vote in this country.

There is no issue of States rights or national rights. There is only the struggle for human rights.

I have not the slightest doubt what will be your answer.

The last time a President sent a civil rights bill to the Congress it contained a provision to protect voting rights in Federal elections. That civil rights bill was passed after 8 long months of debate. And when that bill came to my desk from the Congress for my signature, the heart of the voting provision had been eliminated.

This time, on this issue, there must be no delay, no hesitation and no compromise with our purpose.

We cannot, we must not, refuse to protect the right of every American to vote in every election that he may desire to participate in. And we ought not and we cannot and we must not wait another 8 months before we get a bill. We have already waited a hundred years and more, and the time for waiting is gone.

So I ask you to join me in working long hours—nights and weekends, if necessary—to pass this bill. And I don't make that request lightly. For from the window where I sit with the problems of our country I recognize that outside this chamber is the outraged conscience of a nation, the grave concern of many nations, and the harsh judgment of history on our acts.

We Shall Overcome

But even if we pass this bill, the battle will not be over. What happened in Selma is part of a far larger movement which reaches into every section and State of America. It is the effort of American Negroes to secure for themselves the full blessings of American life.

Their cause must be our cause too. Because it is not just Negroes, but really it is all of us, who must overcome the crippling legacy of bigotry and injustice.

And we shall overcome.

*Source: *Public Papers of the Presidents of the United States: Lyndon B. Johnson, 1965,* volume 1, entry 107, pp. 281–87 (Washington, DC: Government Printing Office, 1966), Lyndon Baines Johnson Library and Museum, http://www.lbjlib.utexas.edu/johnson/archives.hom/ speeches.hom/650315.asp.

Appendix C

Dr. King's Six Principles of Nonviolence Related to Selma

The Six Principles of Nonviolence presented here were extrapolated from Dr. King's book Stride toward Freedom: The Montgomery Story. *King writes about these principles in a powerful and moving essay titled "Pilgrimage to Nonviolence." As I reflect back I can see that the experiences I had in Selma helped me to internalize and practice the principles that are the foundation of nonviolent thinking. Here I'll reflect on the essence of these six principles and illustrate with examples from Selma that are still vividly in my mind today.*

Principle 1. Nonviolence is a way of life for courageous people

Dr. King often talked about how the movement was not for cowards. We somehow need to find the courage deep within ourselves to be able to confront conflict rather than avoid or run away from it. Many times I felt afraid; just going into Selma not knowing what I'd encounter was daunting. But I went there, I stayed, and through my faith and my friends, I worked through the fear. This principle requires that we focus on the heart of the conflict and find ways to deal with the issues and problems in a positive and constructive way, persuading our adversaries of the justice of the cause. For Dr. King this nonviolence principle was never just a tactic to push through his agenda, it was the way he lived every day of his life.

In Selma, an underlying issue of voter registration was the overwhelming fear that the blacks had when dealing with the white system. Blacks feared that whites would feel threatened by large numbers of blacks registering to vote and might retaliate; that they or their family members might lose their jobs, be attacked, or lose their lives. We knew we had to address that fear and help them overcome it. Some individuals took a daring stand in order to help others conquer their paralyzing anxiety by coming to the first mass meeting. Mr. Boynton's life had been an example of courage, and it served to give people strength. When they witnessed the sacrifice of others, it brought out courage that they may not have known existed. Even though the police surrounded the church to intimidate people from coming, some crawled under houses and came through the back way to avoid being seen. But they came.

Principle 2. The Beloved Community is the framework for the future

We should strive to create a community where all people can live together in harmony with no oppressor and no oppressed, with no winner and no loser. We work for the common good and not just personal gain. The first part of this principle, the Beloved Community, calls us to be inclusive, sharing, trusting, and loving. It is not always an absence of conflict, but a positive process in which people attempt to reconcile the conflicts. The second part of the principle looks toward the future with hope and possibility.

One of my personal goals in Selma was to bring people together in a trusting, respectful relationship in order to reduce the fear. I noticed that many of the black leaders were negative toward each other, constantly putting each other down. Some were even snitches for the white power structure and were known as "Uncle Toms." A lack of trust was created among them. The pervasive pessimism was a symptom of deep fear. When people are afraid to take a stand they manufacture excuses, blame others, and rationalize why nothing is being done. One of my strategies was to spread positive remarks that the leaders said about each other. When I saw a key leader on the street, I'd casually share something good that another person had said about him. Gradually, their perceptions of each other changed and they thought more positively about their colleagues. It was at that point they could begin to collaborate and work together to make changes that would have an impact on the future of every individual in Selma.

Principle 3. Attack forces of evil, not persons doing evil

Many communities in the South had certain persons in authority who personified injustice. In Selma it was no different. As difficult as it was, it was necessary to not allow the issue of voter registration to be centered on one individual, and in Selma, that individual was Sheriff Jim Clark. Often it was said, "If we could just get rid of this person or that person, our problem would be solved." Usually that's not the case. Removing a particular individual from office might make a difference, but it typically doesn't solve the problem. Our focus had to be on understanding the root of the problem that produced the oppressive conditions and then how to change the contingencies that fed that condition. The forces of evil that surround the person support the unacceptable behavior. Therefore, our nonviolent approach needed to change the conditions in order to solve the problem.

Principle 4. Accept suffering for the sake of the cause without retaliation to achieve the goal

Some contend that we as human beings by nature are prone to react when attacked, either to defend ourselves or to counterattack. Accepting suffering is not a popular idea for most people. It's more palatable to avoid suffering. In the context of nonviolence this concept has a different meaning. It doesn't mean accepting abuse and punishment with no response. In fact, it requires a response. But that response must be consistent with the goals we seek so that suffering is not in a vacuum but rather in the context of a campaign for change. The first change is within the individual who is the object of the attack. If a person is attacked without a purposeful response then that person could be considered a victim. However, if the person responds without violence but with the power of nonviolence and as part of a strategy to achieve a more just condition, then the suffering becomes the source of strength. Confronting an attacker with courage, steadfastness, determination, and nonviolent resistance creates the potential for arresting the conscience of the assailant. This is why I looked my attacker in the eye when he cracked my head open and knocked me to the ground. I immediately got up and continued to look into his eyes to show him my humanity and to have him recognize me as a human being. The suffering then can become a stimulus to have more determination and to inspire others.

Principle 5. Avoid internal violence of the spirit as well as external physical violence

Sometimes when we use hurtful words we do internal harm to a person's spirit, so it becomes psychological and spiritual violence. Dr. King said that the psychological scars of segregation take longer to heal than physical scars. We also unconsciously do damage to our own spirit when we allow ourselves to become hateful toward others.

In Selma, although there were people who were subservient to whites because they were afraid, I didn't permit others to characterize them as "Uncle Toms" or "Nervous Nellies." That kind of name calling can damage their spirit by projecting negative images on them. In fact, when talking with black leaders, I often paid compliments to others in front of them in order to begin to change the way they thought about those people, to point out positive aspects of others so they would be viewed in a better light.

Principle 6. The arc of the moral universe is long and bends toward justice

In our struggles, sometimes we don't see the end in sight or recognize the goals that are within our grasp. However, we must maintain faith that no matter how dim the hour, how dark the night, or how cloudy the moment, our goal is reachable. People only struggle when they feel they have a chance of achieving their goals. They wouldn't persevere if they thought they had no possibility of success.

Even when we had setbacks, such as the difficulty in finding a place to host the first mass meeting, eventually an opportunity presented itself. In this instance, we seized the unexpected chance to combine our mass meeting with the memorial service for Mr. Boynton. Once again, I saw the truth in this principle, the sense of hope and faith that with continued determination and steady work, justice would ultimately prevail.

Appendix D

Life Dates of Some Persons Referenced in the Book

Rev. Ralph David Abernathy	3/11/1926–4/17/1990
Ella Baker	12/13/1903–12/13/1986
Marion Barry	b. 3/6/1936
Harry Belafonte	b. 3/1/1927
James Bevel	10/19/1936–12/19/2008
Amelia Boynton	b. 8/18/1911
Atty. J. L. Chestnut	12/16/1930–9/30/2008
Sheriff Jim Clark	9/17/1922–6/4/2007
Dorothy Cotton	b. 1930
Benjamin Elton Cox	b. 6/19/1931
Constance Curry	b. 7/19/1933
Atty. John Doar	b. 12/3/1921
Ernest Doyle	b. 3/9/1918
Medgar Evers	7/2/1925–6/12/1963
James Farmer	1/12/1920–7/9/1999
James Forman	10/4/1928–1/10/2005
Marie Foster	10/24/1917–9/6/2003
James Edward Gildersleeve	1918–2004
Jimmie Lee Jackson	12/1938–2/26/1965
Coretta Scott King	4/27/1927–1/30/2006
Dr. Martin Luther King Jr.	1/15/1929–4/4/1968
Jim Lawson	b. 9/22/1928
Jim Letherer	1933–2001
John Lewis	b. 2/21/1940
Rufus Lewis	11/30/1906–1999
Viola Liuzzo	4/11/1925–3/25/1965

Margaret Moore	d. 11/16/2005
Bob Moses	b. 1/23/1935
Diane Nash	b. 5/15/1938
James Edward Orange	10/29/1942–2/16/2008
Father Maurice Ouellet	9/10/1926–7/25/2011
Rev. James Reeb	1/1/1927–3/11/1965
Rev. Frederick Reese	b. 1930
Atty. Solomon Seay	b. 1931
Rev. Fred Shuttlesworth	3/18/1922–10/5/2011
Rev. C. T. Vivian	b. 7/30/1924
Gov. George Wallace	8/25/1919–9/13/1998
Hosea Lorenzo Williams	1/5/1926–11/16/2000
Malcolm X	5/19/1925–2/21/1965
Andrew Young	b. 3/12/1932

Chronology

1820: Selma is founded; Cahawba (south of Selma) is selected as state capital.

1826: Alabama state capital moves from Cahawba to Montgomery.

July 29, 1940: Bernard LaFayette Jr. is born in Tampa, Florida.

May 17, 1954: *Brown v. Board of Education of Topeka:* the U.S. Supreme Court issues a landmark decision that rules having separate public schools for black and white students unconstitutional.

December 1, 1955: Montgomery Bus Boycott begins. Dr. Martin Luther King Jr. launches a successful 381-day protest that leads to desegregation of public transportation.

January 1957: Dr. King and others form the Southern Christian Leadership Conference (SCLC), which becomes an organizing force in the civil rights and nonviolence movement, with Dr. King as its president.

Fall 1958: Bernard LaFayette Jr. begins college in Nashville at American Baptist Theological Seminary.

February 1, 1960: First segregated lunch counter sit-ins at Woolworth's in Greensboro, North Carolina, by four black students, who continue to sit at the counter after being refused service.

February 27, 1960: First arrests for the Nashville Student Movement ongoing lunch counter sit-ins in which Bernard LaFayette Jr. is involved.

April 19, 1960: Bernard LaFayette Jr. with the Nashville Student Movement and more than four thousand others march to city hall and meet with Nashville mayor Ben West. He publicly acknowledges that he feels segregation is morally wrong.

April 1960: Student Nonviolent Coordinating Committee (SNCC) founded at Shaw University, providing a venue of support for young black activists. Bernard LaFayette Jr. is a founding member.

November 9, 1960: John F. Kennedy is elected president.

May 4, 1961: Freedom Rides begin from Washington, D.C., a strategy for black and white activists to challenge local laws that maintain segregation on interstate travel. Bernard LaFayette Jr. later joins as a Freedom Rider.

May 21, 1961: Armed mob of more than two thousand gathers at Selma bus station to attack the Freedom Riders journeying from Montgomery to Jackson; the bus is diverted. Bernard LaFayette Jr. is on the bus and one of those previously attacked at the Montgomery bus station.

November 1, 1961: Interstate Commerce Commission ruling goes into effect desegregating interstate travel.

Spring 1962: Bernard LaFayette Jr. returns to college at Fisk University in Nashville.

November 1962: Bernard LaFayette Jr. marries Colia Liddell, his first wife. He visits Selma to do research.

January 1963: Bernard LaFayette Jr. from SNCC arrives in Selma to direct the Alabama Voter Registration Campaign.

Spring 1963: Bernard LaFayette Jr. trains youth in Birmingham in strategies of nonviolence.

May 2–5, 1963: Children's Crusade in Birmingham: hundreds of schoolchildren march to the mayor's office to protest segregation.

May 14, 1963: First mass meeting and memorial service held for Mr. Boynton.

May 1963: Bernard LaFayette Jr. is arrested on a trumped-up charge of vagrancy as he drives in his car in Selma.

June 10, 1963: President Kennedy sends National Guard to desegregate the University of Alabama after Governor George Wallace blocks the door to the admissions office to prevent black students from enrolling.

June 12, 1963: Tri-state conspiracy: Medgar Evers killed in Mississippi, Benjamin Cox targeted in Louisiana, and Bernard LaFayette Jr. attacked in Alabama.

June 19, 1963: President Kennedy proposes a broad civil rights bill following a June 11 television address urging public support of equal treatment to all, despite race.

Summer 1963: Bernard LaFayette Jr. begins voter registration project in Wilcox County.

August 28, 1963: March on Washington: Dr. King delivers "I Have a Dream" speech and meets with President Kennedy about a civil rights act.

Fall 1963: Bernard LaFayette Jr. returns to college in Nashville and continues his work in Selma on a monthly basis.

September 15, 1963: Birmingham bombing; four girls killed.

October 7, 1963: "Freedom Day": more than three hundred blacks attempt to register to vote in Selma and are arrested.

November 22, 1963: President John F. Kennedy is assassinated.

January 8, 1964: President Lyndon B. Johnson delivers his first State of the Union address and supports the civil rights movement.

January 14, 1964: Colia and Bernard LaFayette Jr.'s first child, James Arthur, is born in Nashville.

Summer 1964: Freedom Summer, the vast effort to register black voters in Mississippi, supported by SNCC, the Congress of Racial Equality (CORE), and other groups. Bernard LaFayette Jr. begins working with Chicago Campaign.

July 2, 1964: Civil Rights Act of 1964 is signed by President Johnson.

July 1964: Judge James A. Hare issues an injunction that forbid groups of three or more to gather.

December 10, 1964: Dr. King awarded the Nobel Peace Prize in Oslo.

January 2, 1965: Dr. King and SCLC come to Selma to join forces with SNCC.

January 22, 1965: Teachers' March in Selma.

February 1, 1965: Dr. King and more than two hundred others arrested in Selma during a voting rights march.

February 2, 1965: Malcolm X speaks at mass meeting in Selma. Bernard LaFayette Jr. helps plan the meeting.

February 9, 1965: Dr. King meets with President Johnson regarding voting rights.

February 21, 1965: Malcolm X is assassinated in New York during a speech.

February 26, 1965: Jimmie Lee Jackson dies from February 18 shooting in Marion, Alabama.

March 3, 1965: Jimmie Lee Jackson's funeral held at Brown Chapel in Selma.

March 7, 1965: First March to Montgomery begins; becomes known as "Bloody Sunday" after marchers are beaten by police on the Edmund Pettus Bridge.

March 9, 1965: Second March to Montgomery begins; becomes known as "Confrontation of Prayer."

March 11, 1965: Rev. James Reeb dies from March 9 beating by white racists.

March 15, 1965: President Johnson gives Special Message to Congress in support of the Voting Rights Act.

March 21, 1965: Third March to Montgomery begins from Selma.

March 24, 1965: "Stars for Freedom" rally at City of St. Jude's.

March 25, 1965: March ends on the steps of the Alabama State Capitol with speech by Dr. King to a crowd of more than twenty-five thousand. Viola Liuzzo is killed by Klansmen while driving marchers back to Selma.

March 1965: Bernard LaFayette Jr. leaves Selma for final time.

April 14, 1965: Colia and Bernard LaFayette Jr.'s second child, Bernard III, is born in Chicago.

August 6, 1965: Voting Rights Act of 1965 is passed.

Notes

1. Preparing for Selma

1. John F. Kennedy, "Inaugural Address, 20 January 1961," John F. Kennedy Presidential Library and Museum, http://www.jfklibrary.org/Asset-Viewer/BqXIEM9F4024ntFl7SVAjA.aspx (accessed August 25, 2012).

2. Supreme Court of the United States, "Brown v. Board of Education, 349 U.S. 294 (1955) (USSC+)," The National Center for Public Policy Research, http://www.nationalcenter.org/cc0725.htm (accessed January 3, 2013).

3. Supreme Court of the United States, "Morgan v. Virginia (No. 704) 184 Va. 24, 34 S.E.2d 491, reversed," Legal Information Institute, Cornell University Law School, http://www.law.cornell.edu/supct/html/historics/USSC_CR_0328_0373_ZS.html (accessed December 14, 2012).

4. "This Month in North Carolina History—April 1947 Freedom Ride," UNC University Libraries, http://www.lib.unc.edu/ncc/ref/nchistory/apr2005/index.html (accessed February 20, 2013).

5. "The Road to Civil Rights: Boynton v. Virginia (1960)," U.S. Department of Transportation, Federal Highway Administration, http://www.fhwa.dot.gov/highwayhistory/road/s25.cfm (accessed October 15, 2012).

6. Howard Zinn, *SNCC: The New Abolitionists,* 3rd ed. (Cambridge, MA: South End, 2002), 32.

7. Cheryl L. Greenburg, *Circle of Trust: Remembering SNCC* (New Brunswick, NJ: Rutgers University Press, 1998), 5.

8. Clayborne Carson, *In Struggle: SNCC and the Black Awakening of the 1960s* (Cambridge, MA: Harvard University Press, 1981), 304.

9. Supreme Court of the United States, "Brown v. Board of Education, 347 U.S. 483 (1954) (USSC+)," The National Center for Public Policy Research, http://www.nationalcenter.org/brown.html (accessed March 27, 2012).

2. Shackles of Fear, Handcuffs of Hopelessness

1. Conversation with Mrs. Boynton, May 2012.

2. "The Road to Civil Rights: Boynton v. Virginia (1960)," U.S. Department of Transportation, Federal Highway Administration, http://www.fhwa.dot.gov/highwayhistory/road/s25.cfm (accessed October 15, 2012).

3. Preparing to Register to Vote

1. "1917 Immigration Act," U.S. Immigration Legislation Online, University of Washington-Bothell Library, http://library.uwb.edu/guides/usimmigration/1917_immigration_act.html (accessed December 20, 2012).

2. Taylor Branch, *Pillar of Fire: America in the King Years 1963–65* (New York: Simon and Schuster, 1999), 77.

4. Central Alabama Heats Up

1. Adam Nossiter, *Of Long Memory: Mississippi and the Murder of Medgar Evers* (Reading, MA: Addison Wesley, 1994), 257.

2. "Maurice F. Ouellet Research Papers, 1963–1968," Amistad Research Center, Tulane University, http://www.amistadresearchcenter.org/archon/?p=collections/controlcard&id=103 (accessed December 22, 2012).

3. Martin Luther King Jr., *Why We Can't Wait* (New York: Signet, 1964), 85.

4. J. R. Moehringer, "Crossing Over," *Los Angeles Times,* August 22, 1999.

5. Mountains and Valleys

1. "East African Independence: A Chronology of Colonization and Independence," African History, About.com, http://africanhistory.about.com/library/bl/bl-Independence-EA2.htm (accessed May 18, 2013).

2. Martin Luther King Jr., "Letter from Birmingham Jail," April 16, 1963, King Papers Project, The Martin Luther King, Jr., Research and Education Institute, Stanford University, http://mlk-kpp01.stanford.edu/index.php/resources/article/annotated_letter_from_birmingham/ (accessed May 18, 2013).

3. John Lewis and Michael D'Orso, *Walking with the Wind: A Memoir of the Movement* (New York: Simon and Schuster, 1999), 226.

4. Martin Luther King Jr., *The Autobiography of Martin Luther King, Jr.* ed. Clayborne Carson (New York: Grand Central, 2001), 226.

5. Taylor Branch, *Pillar of Fire: America in the King Years 1963–65* (New York: Simon and Schuster, 1999), 152.

6. Lyndon B. Johnson, "The President's Inaugural Address," January 20, 1965, *Lyndon B. Johnson XXXVI President of the United States 1963–1969,* no. 27, ed. John Wooley and Gerhard Peters, The American Presidency Project, http://www.presidency.ucsb.edu/ws/index.php?pid=26985 (accessed January 2, 2013).

7. Address at Oberlin College, October 22, 1964, "Continuing the Struggle for Racial Justice—King's Visits to Oberlin," Oberlin College Archives, http://

www.oberlin.edu/external/EOG/BlackHistoryMonth/MLK/MLKmainpage .html (accessed May 18, 2013).

8. Quoted in Clayborne Carson, *In Struggle: SNCC and the Black Awakening of the 1960s* (Cambridge, MA: Harvard University Press, 1981), 260.

9. *Selma: The City and the Symbol,* DVD (CBS News, Films Media Group, 2002).

10. Branch, *Pillar of Fire,* 576.

11. King, *The Autobiography of Martin Luther King, Jr.,* 274.

12. King, *The Autobiography of Martin Luther King, Jr.,* 268.

13. *Eyes on the Prize: America's Civil Rights Years 1954–1965,* narrated by Julian Bond, directed by Henry Hampton, DVD (PBS, 2010).

14. Branch, *Pillar of Fire,* 579.

6. The March from Selma to Montgomery

1. John Lewis and Michael D'Orso, *Walking with the Wind: A Memoir of the Movement* (New York: Simon and Schuster, 1999), 327–28.

2. David Halberstam, *The Children* (New York: Random House, 1998), 510.

3. Halberstam, *The Children,* 507.

4. *King: Go Beyond the Dream to Discover the Man,* narrated by Tom Brokaw, DVD (A&E Television Networks, 2008).

5. Lyndon B. Johnson, "The President's News Conference," March 13, 1965, *Lyndon B. Johnson XXXVI President of the United States 1963–1969,* no. 106, ed. John Wooley and Gerhard Peters, The American Presidency Project, http://www.presidency.ucsb.edu/ws/?pid=26804 (accessed May 18, 2013); Lyndon B. Johnson, "President Lyndon B. Johnson's Special Message to the Congress: The American Promise. March 15, 1965," *Public Papers of the Presidents of the United States: Lyndon B. Johnson, 1965,* vol. 1, entry 107, pp. 281–87 (Washington, DC: Government Printing Office, 1966), Lyndon Baines Johnson Library and Museum, http://www.lbjlib.utexas.edu/johnson/archives.hom/ speeches.hom/650315.asp (accessed October 1, 2009).

6. Martin Luther King Jr., "Our God Is Marching On!," March 25, 1965, King Papers Project, The Martin Luther King, Jr., Research and Education Institute, Stanford University, http://mlk-kpp01.stanford.edu/index.php/ kingpapers/article/our_god_is_marching_on/ (accessed May 18, 2013).

7. Peter Ackerman and Jack DuVall, *A Force More Powerful: A Century of Nonviolent Conflict* (New York: Palgrave, 2000), 333.

7. Reflections on the Alabama Voter Registration Campaign

1. *Eyes on the Prize: America's Civil Rights Years 1954–1965,* narrated by Julian Bond, directed by Henry Hampton, DVD (PBS, 2010).

Bibliography

Ackerman, Peter, and Jack DuVall. *A Force More Powerful: A Century of Nonviolent Conflict*. New York: Palgrave, 2000.

"Application for Registration, Questionnaire and Oaths." Civil Rights Movement Veterans. http://www.crmvet.org/info/litapp.pdf.

Aretha, David. *Selma and the Voting Rights Act (The Civil Rights Movement)*. Greensboro, NC: Morgan Reynolds, 2007.

Arsenault, Raymond. *Freedom Riders: 1961 and the Struggle for Racial Justice*. 2nd ed. New York: Oxford University Press, 2011.

Barton, James. "Conducting Literature Discussions: Lessons Learned from the Teacher Assessment Project." *Teacher Education Quarterly* 18, no. 3 (1991): 97–108.

Branch, Taylor. *At Canaan's Edge: America in the King Years 1965–68*. New York: Simon and Schuster, 2006.

———. *Parting the Waters: America in the King Years 1954–63*. New York: Simon and Schuster, 1989.

———. *Pillar of Fire: America in the King Years 1963–65*. New York: Simon and Schuster, 1999.

Carson, Clayborne. *In Struggle: SNCC and the Black Awakening of the 1960s*. Cambridge, MA: Harvard University Press, 1981.

———. David J. Garrow, Gerald Gill, Vincent Harding, and Darlene Clark Hine, eds. *The Eyes on the Prize Civil Rights Reader: Documents, Speeches, and Firsthand Accounts from the Black Freedom Struggle*. New York: Penguin, 1991.

Chappell, Paul K. *Peaceful Revolution: How We Can Create the Future Needed for Humanity's Survival*. Westport, CT: Easton Studio Press, 2012.

Chestnut, J. L., and Julia Cass. *Black in Selma: The Uncommon Life of J. L. Chestnut, Jr*. N.p. Fire Ant Books, 2007.

Cone, James H. *Martin and Malcolm and America: A Dream or a Nightmare*. Maryknoll, NY: Orbis Books, 1991.

"Continuing the Struggle for Racial Justice—King's Visits to Oberlin." Oberlin College Archives. http://www.oberlin.edu/external/EOG/BlackHistoryMonth/MLK/MLKmainpage.html.

Curry, Constance. *Silver Rights*. Chapel Hill, NC: Algonquin Books, 1995.

Davis, Townsend. *Weary Feet, Rested Souls: A Guided History of the Civil Rights Movement*. New York: W. W. Norton, 1999.

"East African Independence: A Chronology of Colonization and Independence." African History, About.com. http://africanhistory.about.com/library/bl/bl-Independence-EA2.htm.

Eyes on the Prize: America's Civil Rights Years 1954–1965. DVD. Narrated by Julian Bond. Directed by Henry Hampton. PBS, 2010.

Fager, Charles E. *Selma 1965: The March That Changed the South.* New York: Charles Scribner's Sons, 1974.

Fairclough, Adam. *To Redeem the Soul of America: The Southern Christian Leadership Conference and Martin Luther King, Jr.* Athens: University of Georgia Press, 1987.

Farmer, James. *Freedom—When?* New York: Random House, 1965.

Farmer, James, and Don E. Carlton. *Lay Bare the Heart: An Autobiography of the Civil Rights Movement.* New York: Arbor House, 1985.

Fleming, Cynthia G. *In the Shadow of Selma: The Continuing Struggle for Civil Rights in the Rural South.* Lanham, MD: Rowman and Littlefield, 2004.

A Force More Powerful. Directed by Stephen York. DVD. A Force More Powerful Films, 2000.

Forman, James. *The Making of Black Revolutionaries.* New York: Macmillan, 1972.

"40 Lives for Freedom." Civil Rights Memorial Center. http://www.splcenter.org/pdf/static/40lives.pdf.

Friedland, Michael B. *Lift Up Your Voice Like a Trumpet: White Clergy and the Civil Rights and Antiwar Movements, 1954–1973.* Chapel Hill: University of North Carolina Press, 1998.

Garrow, David J. *Bearing the Cross: Martin Luther King, Jr., and the Southern Christian Leadership Conference.* New York: William Morrow, 1986.

———. *Protest at Selma: Martin Luther King, Jr., and the Voting Rights Act of 1965.* New Haven, CT: Yale University Press, 1978.

Giannino, Joanne. "Viola Liuzzo." Unitarian Universalist Historical Society. http://www25.uua.org/uuhs/duub/articles/violaliuzzo.html.

Ginzburg, Ralph. *100 Years of Lynchings.* Baltimore, MD: Black Classic, 1996.

Greenburg, Cheryl L. *Circle of Trust: Remembering SNCC.* New Brunswick, NJ: Rutgers University Press, 1998.

Halberstam, David. *The Best and the Brightest.* New York: Random House, 1972.

———. *The Children.* New York: Random House, 1998.

Hampton, Henry, Steve Fayer, and Sarah Flynn. *Voices of Freedom: An Oral History of the Civil Rights Movement from the 1950s through the 1980s.* New York: Bantam, 1991.

Harding, Vincent. *There Is a River*. New York: Harcourt Brace Jovanovich, 1993.

Harvey, Keith. "Remembering Tony Henry and a Generation of Leaders." *Peace Work: Global Thought and Local Action for Nonviolent Social Change*, no. 384 (April 2008). http://www.peaceworkmagazine.org/print/968.

Johnson, Lyndon B. "President Lyndon B. Johnson's Special Message to the Congress: The American Promise. March 15, 1965." *Public Papers of the Presidents of the United States: Lyndon B. Johnson, 1965*. Vol. 1, entry 107, pp. 281–87. Washington, DC: Government Printing Office. Lyndon Baines Johnson Library and Museum, National Archives and Records Administration. http://www.lbjlib.utexas.edu/johnson/archives.hom/speeches.hom/650315.asp.

———. "The President's Inaugural Address," January 20, 1965. *Lyndon B. Johnson XXXVI President of the United States 1963–1969*, no. 27. Edited by John Wooley and Gerhard Peters. The American Presidency Project. http://www.presidency.ucsb.edu/ws/index.php?pid=26985.

———. "The President's News Conference," March 13, 1965. *Lyndon B. Johnson XXXVI President of the United States 1963–1969*, no. 106. Edited by John Wooley and Gerhard Peters. The American Presidency Project. http://www.presidency.ucsb.edu/ws/?pid=26804

Kennedy, John F. "Inaugural Address, 20 January 1961." John F. Kennedy Presidential Library and Museum. http://www.jfklibrary.org/Asset-Viewer/BqXIEM9F4024ntFl7SVAjA.aspx.

King, Martin Luther, Jr. "Letter from Birmingham Jail." April 16, 1963. King Papers Project. The Martin Luther King, Jr., Research and Education Institute, Stanford University, http://mlk-kpp01.stanford.edu/index.php/resources/article/annotated_letter_from_birmingham/.

———. "Our God Is Marching On!" March 25, 1965. King Papers Project. The Martin Luther King, Jr., Research and Education Institute, Stanford University. http://mlk-kpp01.stanford.edu/index.php/kingpapers/article/our_god_is_marching_on/.

———. *Strength to Love*. New York: Harper and Row, 1964.

———. *Stride toward Freedom: The Montgomery Story*. New York: Harper and Row, 1958.

———. *The Autobiography of Martin Luther King, Jr.* Edited by Clayborne Carson. New York: Grand Central, 2001.

———. *Why We Can't Wait*. New York: Signet, 1964.

King: Go Beyond the Dream to Discover the Man. Narrated by Tom Brokaw. DVD. A&E Television Networks, 2008.

Leonard, Richard D. *Call to Selma: Eighteen Days of Witness*. Boston, MA: Skinner House Books, 2002.

Lerna, Gerda, ed. *Black Women in White America: A Documentary History.* New York: Vintage Books, 1992.

Lewis, John, and Michael D'Orso. *Walking with the Wind: A Memoir of the Movement.* New York: Simon and Schuster, 1999.

"Malcolm and the Civil Rights Movement." Malcolm X, Make It Plain. American Experience. http://pbs.org/wgbh/amex/malcolmx/peopleevents/e_civilrights.html.

"Malcolm X in Selma, Alabama (February 4, 1965)." YouTube. http://www.youtube.com/watch?v=mg5uQQw2leU.

"Maurice F. Ouellet Research Papers, 1963–1968." Amistad Research Center, Tulane University. http://www.amistadresearchcenter.org/archon/?p=collections/controlcard&id=103.

Mighty Times: The Children's March. DVD. Hudson and Houston. A Project of the Southern Poverty Law Center. Montgomery, AL: Teaching Tolerance, 2005.

Moehringer, J. R. "Crossing Over." *Los Angeles Times,* August 22, 1999.

"1917 Immigration Act." U.S. Immigration Legislation Online. University of Washington-Bothell Library. http://library.uwb.edu/guides/usimmigration/1917_immigration_act.html.

Nossiter, Adam. *Of Long Memory: Mississippi and the Murder of Medgar Evers.* Reading, MA: Addison Wesley, 1994.

Perry, Bruce, ed. *Malcolm X: The Last Speeches.* Atlanta, GA: Pathfinder, 1992.

Raines, Howard. *My Soul Is Rested: Movement Days in the Deep South Remembered.* New York: Penguin, 1983.

"The Road to Civil Rights: Boynton v. Virginia (1960)." U.S. Department of Transportation, Federal Highway Administration. http://www.fhwa.dot.gov/highwayhistory/road/s25.cfm.

Robinson, Amelia B. *Bridge across Jordon.* Washington, DC: Schiller Institute, 1991.

Selma: The City and the Symbol. DVD. CBS News Films Media Group, 2002.

"Southern Regional Council Papers, 1944–1968." King Collection, Robert W. Woodruff Library, Atlanta University Center. http://www.auctr.edu/rwwl/Home/tabid/448/Default.aspx.

Stanton, Mary. *From Selma to Sorrow: The Life and Death of Viola Liuzzo.* Athens: University of Georgia Press, 2000.

Supreme Court of the United States. "Brown v. Board of Education, 347 U.S. 483 (1954) (USSC+)." The National Center for Public Policy Research. http://www.nationalcenter.org/brown.html.

———. "Brown v. Board of Education, 349 U.S. 294 (1955) (USSC+)."

The National Center for Public Policy Research. http://www.national-center.org/cc0725.htm.

———. "Morgan v. Virginia (No. 704) 184 Va. 24, 34 S.E.2d 491, reversed." Legal Information Institute, Cornell University Law School. http://www.law.cornell.edu/supct/html/historics/USSC_CR_0328_0373_ZS.html.

"This Month in North Carolina History—April 1947 Freedom Ride." UNC University Libraries. http://www.lib.unc.edu/ncc/ref/nchistory/apr2005/index.html.

Vaughn, Wally G. *The Selma Campaign, 1963–1965: The Decisive Battle of the Civil Rights Movement.* Dover, MA: Majority Press, 2006.

"Voting Rights: Are *You* 'Qualified' to Vote? Take a 'Literacy Test' to Find Out." Veterans of the Civil Rights Movement. http://www.crmvet.org/info/lithome.htm.

Webb-Christburg, Sheyann, Rachel West Nelson, and Frank Sikora. *Selma, Lord, Selma: Girlhood Memories of the Civil Rights Days.* 2nd ed. Tuscaloosa: University of Alabama Press, 1997.

Young, Andrew. *An Easy Burden: The Civil Rights Movement and the Transformation of America.* 2nd ed. New York: HarperCollins, 2008.

———. *A Way Out of No Way: The Spiritual Memoirs of Andrew Young.* New York: Thomas Nelson, 1994.

Zinn, Howard. *A People's History of the United States.* New York: HarperCollins, 2010.

———. *SNCC: The New Abolitionists.* 3rd ed. Cambridge, MA: South End, 2002.

———. *The Zinn Reader: Writings on Disobedience and Democracy.* New York: Seven Stories, 2009.

Index